JN260663

# はしがき

　本書では，英文を書いたり，話したりする際によく間違えてしまう英文法の事項を，項目別に 15 の Chapter に割り振って取り上げている。各 Chapter では，最初は英文構成において必要な事項及び誤りやすい点に関して，具体例や例文を交えて簡潔に解説が施してあり，次に，この解説に有機的に結びつく練習問題（正誤問題や空欄補充問題等）を解き，これを通して解説の内容の定着を図れるようになっている。最後にまとめとして短い英作文を行い，犯しやすい誤りを克服するとともに，英語の基礎的作文能力を涵養するという構成になっている。

　英文を書く場合，英語の学習者が間違えてしまうものとしては句読法に関するものが多いように思われるため，本書では英文構成の最も基礎的な事項である句読法を最初の Chapter に配置した。その後の Chapter は，間違えやすい英文法の事項を品詞別に配置している。また，英文構成には語彙力も必要となってくるため，最後に英語を書く際，覚えておくと役に立つ語彙をジャンル別に問題形式で付録として付けてあり，こうした問題を通して，語彙の面からも英文法や英作文の学習をサポートできるように構成されている。

　本書は，大学の英語の専門の授業だけでなく，英語を専門としない学習者に対しても使えるように工夫した。本書を用いて，英文法の基礎を身につけるだけでなく，TOEIC 等の検定試験の文法事項の対策用としても使用して頂ければ幸甚です。

2008 年　春

宗 正 佳 啓

# 目　次

はしがき ……………………………………………………………… i

Chapter 1　句読法 ………………………………………………… 1

Chapter 2　名詞(1) ……………………………………………… 9

Chapter 3　名詞(2) ……………………………………………… 13

Chapter 4　冠詞(1) ……………………………………………… 18

Chapter 5　冠詞(2) ……………………………………………… 22

Chapter 6　冠詞(3) ……………………………………………… 26

Chapter 7　動詞(1) ……………………………………………… 31

Chapter 8　動詞(2) ……………………………………………… 36

Chapter 9　形容詞 ………………………………………………… 41

Chapter 10　副　詞 ……………………………………………… 46

Chapter 11　前置詞 ……………………………………………… 52

Chapter 12　関係代名詞 ………………………………………… 56

Chapter 13　準動詞 ……………………………………………… 61

Chapter 14　比　較 ……………………………………………… 67

Chapter 15　その他注意すべき構文 …………………………… 71

## 語彙

日用品…76　　文房具…76　　食品…76　　鉄道…77　　犯罪(1)…77

犯罪(2)…77　　犯罪(3)…77　　科学技術…78　　化学(1)…78　　化学(2)…78

電話…79　　気候(1)…79　　気候(2)…79　　気候(3)…79　　郵便(1)…80

郵便(2)…80　　郵便(3)…80　　学校(1)…81　　学校(2)…81　　学校(3)…81

学問(1)…81　　学問(2)…82　　病名(1)…82　　病名(2)…82　　病名(3)…82

医者…83　　人体…83　　職業(1)…83　　職業(2)…84　　海外旅行(1)…84

海外旅行(2)…84　　政治(1)…85　　政治(2)…85　　政治(3)…85　　政治(4)…85

経済(1)…86　　経済(2)…86　　経済(3)…86　　宗教(1)…87　　宗教(2)…87

ビジネス(1)…87　　ビジネス(2)…87　　ビジネス(3)…88　　図形(1)…88

図形(2)…88　　数学(1)…88　　数学(2)…89　　数学(3)…89　　数学(4)…89

グラフ…90

練習問題の解答……………………………………………………………………91

# Chapter 1 句 読 法

　英文を構成する際には，様々な句読点を加えることで文や語句の境界を明らかにし，意味を伝えやすくします。以下，英語の句読点の基礎的な使い方を解説しておきます。

1．終止符（period/ full stop）〈 . 〉の使い方
　① 文または発話文の終わり
　　I wonder if it will rain tomorrow.
　　Nice to see you.
　② 語句の省略
　　50 B. C. (Before Christ) / 60 A. D. (Anno Domini) / Dr. Johnson (Doctor)
　　U. S. A. (United States of America)
　③ 少数点，通貨の単位
　　35.23　＄6.20
　④ 論文の各章の表題や見出しに番号を付ける場合，その番号の後や参考文献の各項目の後
　　V. Wh-movement
　　Chomsky, Noam (1993) "A Minimalist Program for Linguistic Theory," *The View from Building 20*, ed. by Kenneth Hale and Samuel Jay Keyser, 1-52, MIT Press, Cambridge, MA.

2．感嘆符（exclamation mark）〈！〉の使い方
　① 感嘆文の後
　　What a nice scenery!

② 感嘆詞の後

Oh, my God!

③ 激しい感情を表す場合

Nonsense!

④ 祈願を表す場合

May God save the Queen!

3．疑問符 (question mark)〈?〉の使い方

① 疑問文

Where do you come from?

② 驚きを表す場合や相手に念を押す場合

He becomes a doctor?（彼が医者になったって）

You've done it?（それをやったのだね）

③ 相手の言葉を聞き返す場合

He did what?（彼が何をしたって）

④ 付加疑問文

That mountain is beautiful, isn't it?

4．コンマ (comma)〈,〉の使い方

① 住所の各項目を区切る場合

He lives in Chicago, Illinois.

② 日付で年と日を区切る

April 20, 2004

③ 呼びかけの場合

Hey, are you ready?

④ 一つの and または or を使って三つ以上の語，句，文を並べる場合

A, B, and C ／ A, B, or C

⑤ 従属接続詞によって形成される節が，主節よりも先に生じる場合両者

を区切るために使う。

When I was walking along the street, I met a friend of mine.

⑥ 二つ以上の独立節を等位接続詞でつなぐ場合（and, but, or, so, nor, yet, for 等）

He was rich, but he was not happy.

He was ill, so he didn't go out.

⑦ 接続詞的な働きをする副詞または副詞句がある場合

However, he was one of our important persons in the meeting.

He was, however, one of our important persons in the meeting.

■この種の副詞には次のようなものがある。

however, nevertheless, otherwise, therefore, accordingly, consequently, likewise, moreover, furthermore, besides, indeed, for example, in other words, on the contrary, that is to say, first of all, in the first place, etc.

⑧ 非制限用法の場合

関係代名詞または関係副詞以下の節が非制限用法を表すときはコンマを入れる。

Mt. Everest, which lies in the Himalayas, is the highest mountain in the world.

He has gone to Italy, where his brother is working.

■分詞句の場合も同様である。

Charles Dickens, born in 1812, wrote the novel *A Christmas Carol*.

⑨ 同格を表す場合

George W. Bush, president of the United States, sent troops to Iraq.

⑩ 挿入語句の前後に入れ，文全体や他の語句と区別する場合

His lecture, I think, is interesting and full of wit.

## 5．コロン〈:〉の使い方

前述のものに対して例を挙げたり，説明を加えたり，文を導入する場合に

用いる。
「つまり」「すなわち」といった意味を持つ。
① 文の内容に対して具体的な説明を加える場合
He admired three famous American authors: R. W. Emerson, W. Whitman, and H. D. Thoreau.
② 長い引用文を導入する場合
Let us consider this quotation from *Macbeth*: "Tomorrow, and tomorrow, and tomorrow creeps in this petty pace …"
③ 論文の副題を付ける場合
Multiple Interrogatives: A Minimalist Approach
④ 時間と分，章と節を区切る場合
7:30 p.m. / John 11:2 （ヨハネの福音書11章2節）

6．セミコロン〈；〉の使い方
コンマより区切りが強く，ピリオドでは弱すぎる場合に用いる。
① 二つ以上の独立節を接続詞（and, but, or, so, for, nor, yet など）なしでつなぐ場合
Shakespeare wrote his play in blank verse; D. H. Lawrence wrote his poems in free verse.
② 二つの独立節を接続詞的な副詞でつなぐ場合
There had been a great deal of rain; consequently, the banks collapsed in several places.

7．ダッシュ〈—〉の使い方
① 前文の要素を説明したり言い換えたりする場合
He is about my age, but he is paid $400 an hour — twice as much as my wage.
② 文の途中に説明を加える場合

On my birthday － May 15 － he always gives me a present.

8．丸かっこ〈( )〉の使い方

文中に注釈，補足，説明を加える場合

Modern science (especially technology) has produced a lot of electric appliances.

9．アポストロフィー〈'〉の使い方

① 所有格を表したり，文字の短縮形を表す場合

John's father / I'm (I am)

② 文字や数字を複数形にする場合

There are three e's in the word employee.

the five A's（五つのＡ）

10．ハイフン〈-〉の使い方

① 複合語の場合

broad-minded

② 接頭辞の場合

ex-convict / non-native

③ 21から99までの数字や分数の分子と分母の間

twenty-one / ninety-nine / one-fifth / two-thirds

④ 範囲，期間を表す場合

See pages 13-15. Alexander Pope (1688-1744)

11．引用符〈" "〉の使い方

① 文を引用したり会話の部分を表す場合

He said, "I need not learn."

■ピリオドを付すのは引用符内のみであり外には付けない。ただし疑問

符は疑問文が引用文であるか主文であるかで次のように区別する。

She asked, "Are you all right?"　Did he say, "I'm from Germany"?

また引用部分の中にさらに引用がある場合その部分は〈''〉を使用する。

He said," 'Syntax' has a special meaning in grammar."

② 言葉を定義する場合

Syntax means "the rules of grammar which are used for ordering and connecting words to form phrases or sentences."

③ 論文，詩，歌などの題を表す場合

My favorite poem is "The Falling of the Leaves."

## 12. 大文字の使い方

① 文や発話文の最初の文字

He said, "Hi, How are you?"

② 固有名詞や月，曜日，祭日の最初

John / London / May / Monday / Easter

③ 書物，雑誌，新聞，小説，映画，芸術作品の表題

*Wuthering Heights* / *The Observer* / *Linguistic Inquiry* / *Terminator*

## 13. イタリック（斜字体）の使い方

① 文中のある語句を強調する場合

The dead line of this application is *the end of the month*.

② 外国語を表す場合

*Hara-kiri* is given as English in this dictionary.

③ 書物，雑誌，新聞，小説，映画，芸術作品の表題

上記12の③参照

## 練習問題

I．次の英文の必要な所に句読点を入れよ。

1. Don't you think you have had enough steak
2. Would you like some coffee
3. If you hurry up you will be in time for the train
4. My youngest uncle who lives in New York is a doctor
5. I lived in Tampa Florida
6. Gentlemen please
7. He hoped that she would come with his mother and that they would make an apple pie for him
8. This book if you read it well will greatly benefit you
9. On May 7 1945 Germany proclaimed the unconditional surrender to the Allies
10. In 1995 he married Jane a woman seven or eight years older than himself
11. He tried to solve the problem for he could not go ahead without a solution
12. He sought a solution however all his efforts failed
13. Water consists of two elements oxygen and hydrogen
14. He cried Help me out
15. Before dinner on the terrace they spent an hour
16. Little can be said for the book the author doesn't know rhetoric
17. He wrote more than fifty plays in verse one of the most frequently used forms in the 17th century
18. The village where he lives is famous for its production of orange
19. *Atami* where I went for change of air a few years ago is within reach of Tokyo
20. He bought a new house which he has lately moved into

Ⅱ．日本語に合うように（　　　）内に適切な英語を入れなさい。
1．「最近胃の具合が良くありません。」「それはお気の毒に。」
　　"Something is (　　　) with my stomach these days." "That's too (　　　)."
2．シェイクスピアはエリザベス朝において最も人気のある劇作家であり，人気において彼に匹敵するものはほとんどいなかった。
　　Shakespeare was the most (　　　) dramatist in the Elizabethan age, and few dramatists in the world could (　　　) him in popularity.
3．イギリスはイングランド，スコットランド，ウエールズ，北アイルランドの4つの異なる国で成り立っている。
　　The United Kingdom is (　　　) up of four different regions : England, Scotland, Wales, and Northern Ireland.
4．次の角を右に曲がれば左に駅が見えます。
　　(　　　) to the right at the next corner, and you will (　　　) the station in the left side.
5．太郎は1998年3月5日に東京を発ちニューヨークへ向かった。
　　Taro (　　　) Tokyo and (　　　) for New York March 5, 1998.

Ⅲ．次の日本語を英語にしなさい。
1．この食べ物は食事を減らせない人々のために開発されました。
2．私は温泉で有名な大分県へよく行きます。
3．アメリカの有名な小説家ヘミングウェイは長編小説だけでなく短編小説も書いた。
4．彼は「私の立場にあったらあなたも同じことをしただろう」と言った。
5．あなたは夕食前に忘れずに薬を飲みましたか。そうでなければ今飲んだほうがいいですよ。

## Chapter 2　名　　詞(1)

1．「～のうちの1つ」の注意点

　「～のうちの1つ」の意味を表す場合 one of の後の名詞は常に複数形になる。

　　She is one of my best friends.
　　This is one of my favorite things.

2．不可算名詞の注意点

　不可算名詞はいつも単数形で使われ冠詞の a はつけない。不可算名詞としては次のようなものがある。

　　advise, baggage, clothing, evidence, food, fruit, furniture, equipment, homework, housework, information, knowledge, mail, merchandise, postage, slang

3．常に複数形として扱われる名詞

　chopsticks, glasses, gloves, pants, trousers, jeans, pajamas, scissors などは常に複数形として扱われる。cattle, clergy, police は複数形にはなっていないが常に複数名詞として扱われる。people も通常複数名詞として扱われるが，a people, peoples となると民族，国民の意味になる。

　　The police are investigating the murder case.
　　These pants are very expensive.

　■ clergy や police に対してそれぞれの個人を表す場合は clergyman, policeman となる。

### 4．物質名詞の数え方

物質名詞は直接数えられないため容器や量の単位を用いて数える。

a bottle of wine, three spoonfuls of sugar, two pounds of pork, three grams of gold, a cake of soap, a slice of bread, three sheets of paper, a lump of sugar

### 5．複数形で違う意味を持つ名詞

複数形になることで特殊な意味を持つ名詞がある。

air → airs（気取り）　　content → contents（内容）　　custom → customs（関税）　　damage → damages（損害賠償）　　letter → letters（文学）　　manner → manners（作法）　　part → parts（地方）

### 6．固有名詞にaが付く場合

固有名詞にaが付くと「～のような人」,「～という人」,「～家の人」という意味になる。

a Shakespeare（シェイクスピアのような人）　　a Mr. Jones（ジョーンズさんという人）　　a Yamada（山田家の人）

### 7．客を表す名詞

客を表す名詞にはcustomer, guest, clientなどがあるが，それぞれデパートや店の客，ホテルや旅館などの客，弁護士などの客を意味する。

### 8．友達を表す名詞

boyfriendやgirlfriendは通常「恋人」を意味する。ただの異性の友達の場合はmale friendやfemale friendのように言う。また，loverは「恋人」でも不倫相手を意味する場合がある。

## 9. 男性を表す -or, -er, 女性を表す -ess

男優は actor, 女優の場合は actress であるが, 店の経営者や支配人は master ではなく, 男性の場合は manager, 女性の場合は manageress という。

## 10. 相手を表す名詞

仲間を表す場合, companion または partner であるが, スポーツなどの競技の相手を意味する「敵」は opponent という。


## 練習問題

Ⅰ. 次の（　）内から正しい語を選びなさい。
1. He is the greatest man of (a letter, letters) in this country.
2. He cannot read a paper without (glass, glasses).
3. It is bad (manner, manners) to make noises at table.
4. He ordered (two furnitures, two pieces of furniture) from the shop.
5. This company offers goods to its (guests, customers) at a special price.

Ⅱ. 次の各文の誤りを訂正しなさい。
1. My father gave me a good advice.
2. Yesterday I met one of my old friend.
3. Please give me three chalks.
4. We got through custom before we were admitted into the country.
5. The clergy is opposing the bill.

Ⅲ. 日本語に合うように（　）内に適切な英語を入れなさい。
1. そのテニスの選手は相手を見くびって負けてしまった。
   The tennis player (　　) the opponent and lost.

2．彼は地方に転勤することになったので，家族を東京に残しました。
　　He was transferred to (　　　), so he left his family (　　　) in Tokyo.
3．食べる草がなかったので牛の群れは死にかかっていた。
　　The cattle were (　　　) because they had no (　　　) to eat.
4．明日の数学の宿題をしなければならないので今日は外出できません。
　　I cannot go out today because I have to do my math homework (　　　) tomorrow.
5．機内へは何個手荷物を持ち込めますか。
　　How many pieces of (　　　) can I take (　　　) the airplane with me?

Ⅳ．次の日本語を英語にしなさい。
1．食事中に騒がしくすることは無作法ですよ。
2．彼はコーヒーに砂糖を3杯入れた。
3．そのめがねをかけている生徒は年の割にはとても背が高い。
4．先日の洪水はその町に多大の損害を与えた。
5．彼は日本で最大の文学者である。

## Chapter 3 名　　詞(2)

1．「旅」，「旅行」を表す語

　「旅」，「旅行」を意味する語にはいろいろある。travel は一般的な意味の旅行を表すが，イギリス英語では外国旅行を表す。trip は長期・短期の旅行を表すがイギリス英語では短期の旅行を表す。tour は組織的に組まれた計画的な旅行で，journey は通常長距離の陸路の旅行を，excursion は修学旅行など団体での旅行を，flight は飛行機による旅行を表す。また，以下のように動詞の種類によってはその目的語になれないものもある。

　　○ I make / take a trip.
　　× I make a travel.

2．頭は head で表せるか

　head は頭だけを表すと考えてしまうことが多いが，これは頭だけでなく首も含めた語である。賛成を表す場合「首を縦に振る」というが英語では nod one's head といい，拒否を表す「首を横に振る」は shake one's head という。

3．単数と複数の名詞

　人の集団を示す名詞は，単数形および複数形の動詞とともに用いることができる。こうした名詞が一つの単位として考えられる場合は，単数として扱われ，人々の集団と考えらる場合は，複数として扱われる。こうした名詞には team, committee, family, government, firm 等がある。

　　The family is / are taking a trip.
　　The team is / are going to win.

## 4．観客，聴衆を表す名詞

観客，聴衆を表す名詞 audience は単数形および複数形の動詞とともに用いることができるが，観客，聴衆の多さまたは少なさを表す場合はそれぞれ large, small を付けて表す。

　The audience was / were mostly old people.

　There was a large / small audience.

## 5．サラリーマンは適切な英語か

サラリーマンや OL は和製英語でありこのままでは英語として通じない。これらに相当する表現はそれぞれ office worker, female worker であり，文で表すと以下のようになる。

　My father works in an office.

　My father works for a foreign-affiliated company in Tokyo.

## 6．「口」に関連する表現

「口」を表す英語は mouth であるが，「口が軽い」，「口が悪い」，「口をつむぐ」，「口が利けない」，「口を滑らす」などは mouth ではなく tongue を使いそれぞれ，have a loose tongue, have a bitter tongue, hold one's tongue, lose one's tongue, make a slip of the tongue という。

## 7．「目」に関連する表現

「目」を含む表現で catch one's eye（目を引く），keep an eye open（目を皿のようにして探す），have one's eye on（目をつける），cannot believe one's eye（目を疑う）などは eye でよいが，次のような表現には eye を使わない。

　have good sight（目がよい），have a bad time（ひどい目にあう），I'll show you.（目に物みせてやる），come to mind（目に浮かぶ），favor（目をかける）

## 8．所有格の注意点

名詞の所有格は通常生物を表す語には 's をつけて表し，無生物を表す名詞には of を用いるが，時間，距離，金額，重量を表す名詞には 's で表す。

today's news paper, five miles' distance, five dollars' book, one kilogram's weight

## 9．副詞的な働きを持つ句

with ＋抽象名詞が副詞の働きを持つ場合がある。

with ease (easily), with difficulty (barely), with calmness (calmly), with kindness (kindly), with rapidity (rapidly), with warmth (warmly)

## 10．代名詞の注意点

2つあるもののうち1つは one で，もう一方は the other で表す。3つの場合は1つは one，もう1つは another，残りの1つは the other になる。たくさんあるもののうち1つは one，残り全部は the others になる。たくさんあるもののうちいくつかは some，残り全部は the others となる。また，some～others... が「～するものもあれば…するものもある」という意味をもつ場合がある。

Some of the students like him and others hate him.

また，another は数としては単数であるが，another ten minutes（もう10分）のよう複数名詞の前に置いて「もう～」の意味を持つ場合がある。


**練習問題**

Ⅰ．次の（　）内から正しい語を選びなさい。
1．One of his parents is a doctor, and (the other, another) is a nurse.
2．I'm planning to (do, take) a trip next month.

3. To speak is one thing and to write is (the other, another).
4. I had a bad (eye, time) at that party.
5. I lost my (mouth, tongue) when she spoke evil of my teacher.

Ⅱ．次の各文の誤りを訂正しなさい。
1. He climbed the mountain with an ease.
2. A good idea came to my head last night.
3. He shook his neck in disapproval in discussing the pay raise at the meeting.
4. Please keep this wine in this refrigerator for other ten minutes.
5. There were large audience in the concert hall.

Ⅲ．日本語に合うように（　　）内に適切な英語を入れなさい。
1. 10人の競争者のうち3人は賞を得たが，その他は皆賞を得なかった。
   Three of the ten (　　) won prizes; the (　　) got nothing.
2. 外に出かけるのが好きな人もあればテレビを見て家にいるのが好きな人もいる。
   Some people are (　　) of going out; others prefer staying (　　) to watch TV.
3. 私の意見は大抵の人の意見とは異なっています。
   My opinion (　　) from (　　) of most people.
4. 彼は自分の時計を目を皿のようにして探したが出てこなかった。
   He tried (　　) to find his watch with keeping an eye (　　).
5. 彼は商用で今アメリカにいます。
   He has gone to the United States on (　　).

Ⅳ．次の日本語を英語にしなさい。
1. 昨日彼がプレゼントをくれた時，私は目を疑いました。

2．彼は口が軽いので思っていることを何でも言わない方がいいですよ。
3．「次の日曜日田舎にハイキングに行きませんか。」
　　「次の日曜日は都合が悪いです。」
4．彼女はOLをしていたころ万一に備えて500万円貯めました。
5．彼は仰向けになって本を読んでいました。

# Chapter 4　冠　　詞(1)

## 1. 冠詞の a が付く場合
　名詞が数えられる名詞で不定冠詞 a(n) が付く場合は，その名詞が明確な形を持ったものであり，付かない場合はその名詞が明確な形を持たないものである。
　　　I bought a chicken. (chicken は1つの単一体を表している)
　　　I like chicken.（chicken は1つの単一体を表さず鶏の肉を指している）

## 2. 総称を表す冠詞
　a(n) は「〜というもの」という総称的な意味を持つ場合がある。
　　　A tiger is a dangerous animal.
　　　A horse is a domestic animal.

## 3. 不定冠詞 a のいろいろ
　a(n) が「ある〜」，「同じ〜」，「〜につき」といった意味を持つ場合がある。
　　　on a fine day（ある晴れた日に）　　These are all of a kind.（これらはすべて同じ種類である）　　twice a day（一日につき2回）

## 4. 不定冠詞 a が目的語についた場合
　動詞の目的語の位置に可算名詞を置く場合，それに a(n) が付くのは「1つの〜」という解釈が可能な場合のみである。
　　　× I like a tomato.
　　　○ I like tomatoes.
　　　○ I ate a tomato.

## 5．定冠詞の使い方

前に一度出た名詞をさす場合や，その場の状況や既存情報として話者と聞き手が何をさしているか明確な場合，その名詞には the が付く。

They gave me an old house 20 years ago. But I still live in the house.

Please, open the door.

## 6．関係代名詞節と定冠詞

関係代名詞節や前置詞句が後ろについて限定されている名詞には the が付く。

The wines that France produces are among the best in the world.

The car John bought has been stolen.

the President of USA ／ the house on the corner

## 7．無冠詞の名詞の分布

a kind of や a sort of の後ろには無冠詞の名詞がくる。

It's a kind of magic.

I bought a new sort of car

She is not the sort of person to do such a thing.

## 8．慣用表現としての the ＋名詞

慣用表現として the をつける名詞がある。

the rest of ～（～の残り）　　the country（田舎）　　the measles（はしか）　　the point（要点）　　the suburbs（郊外）

## 9．of ＋抽象名詞

of ＋抽象名詞は形容詞の働きを持つが，その抽象名詞には冠詞はつけない。

○ This theory is of importance to us.

× This theory is of an importance to us.

10. 不定冠詞＋固有名詞

a(n) の後に製造会社名がくるとその製品を意味することがある。

　　a Toyota（トヨタの車）　　a Ford（フォード社の車）


**練習問題**

Ⅰ．次の（　）内に適当な冠詞を入れなさい。
1．He bought (　　) TV yesterday.
2．He earns ￥10,000 (　　) day.
3．We bought a used car, but (　　) motor was brand new.
4．He has lived in (　　) country for (　　) long time.
5．I dropped (　　) purse with some money in it. (　　) purse was found out, but (　　) money was gone.

Ⅱ．次の各文の誤りを訂正しなさい。
1．What kind of a book do you have?
2．We ate a chicken at the restaurant.
3．The car can run 100 miles the hour.
4．We are all of the age.
5．An eagle is a bird of the prey.

Ⅲ．日本語に合うように（　　）内に適切な英語を入れなさい。
1．彼は一週間に一度家にいる彼の両親に手紙を書きます。
　　He (　　) to his parents at home (　　) a week.
2．私たちのうちビルはアメリカ人で残りはドイツ人です。

Bill is (　　) and the rest of (　　) are German.
３．彼はそのようなことをする人ではない。
　　He is not the (　　) of man to do (　　) a thing.
４．太陽が東から昇り西に沈むことは真実である。
　　It is true that (　　) sun rises in (　　) east and sets in the west.
５．日増しに寒くなり，日も短くなる秋の初めは天気は比較的安定しています。
　　At the (　　) of autumn when it gets colder day by day and the days get (　　), we usually have settled weather.

## Ⅳ．次の日本語を英語にしなさい。
１．私たちが住んでいる地球はまるく，その表面は海と陸とで成っています。
２．彼に一度会ってみると彼が誠実な人であることが分かりますよ。
３．鯨というものは哺乳動物である。
４．彼は傘を電車に置いてきたのかバスに置いてきたのかはっきりしないんだと言った。
５．お金を多く持っていようが少なかろうがそんなことはとるに足らないことである。問題なのは今持っているお金をどのように使うかである。

# Chapter 5　冠　　詞(2)

## 1．冠詞の位置
　冠詞は単独では用いられず，必ず名詞の前に置かれる。ただし形容詞が名詞を修飾する場合冠詞は形容詞の前に置かれ，さらに副詞がその形容詞を修飾する場合冠詞はその副詞の前に置かれる。
　　a young man / a fairly old man
　■この語順は感嘆文の場合や all, both, double, half, many, quite, rather, such, so, as, too が名詞の前にくる場合変化するので注意を要する。
　　What a nice day! / How wonderful a day! / all the bad men / both the students / at double the cost / half an hour / many a friend / such a fast car / rather a hot day / in so short a time / as fat a man as you / too long a day

## 2．一般的な意味を持つ名詞と冠詞
　名詞が一般的な意味で使われているときは名詞の前に the を付けない。但し名詞が特定なものを指すときは the を付ける。
　　I like music.
　　This is the music I played yesterday.

## 3．食事を表す名詞と冠詞
　食事を表す名詞の前には a や the といった冠詞は付けない。
　　I had lunch in that restaurant today.
　　Why don't we have dinner now?
　ただし食事を表す名詞の前に形容詞がある場合その前に a を付け，また食

事を表す名詞の後にそれを限定する節などがくると the が付く。

 We had a nice dinner last night.

 The lunch she cooked for us was very nice.

## 4．定冠詞 the が生じる環境

 名詞を修飾する最上級の形容詞の前には the が付くが，序数が伴った名詞の前や right, wrong, same, only, sole といった語の前には常に the が付く。

 the first flight / the best answer / the right answer / the wrong answer / the same mistake / the only person / the sole survivor

## 5．体と定冠詞の the

 体の部分を表す名詞には the が付く。

 He pulled her by the arm.

 He banged himself on the forehead.

## 6．役割や役職に関する名詞と冠詞

 単数名詞が述語になっている場合冠詞が付くが，述語が特定の役割や役職に関する名詞である場合付かないこともある。

 Tom is an engineer.

 John F. Kennedy was (the) President of the United States.

 He was (the) chairperson of this committee.

## 7．交通手段や通信手段と冠詞

 交通手段や通信手段を表す名詞には冠詞は付かない。

 by car / by bus / by train / by plane / by boat / by radio / by telephone / by mail

 ただし「～で」という交通手段を表さず，ある乗り物に乗っている状態を表す場合冠詞が付く。

in a car / in a plane / in a train

## 8. 時間に関する語と冠詞

日中や夜を表す名詞には特定な場合を除いて冠詞は付かない。

at sunrise / at daybreak / at sunset / by night / at night / before dark / after midnight

ただし次のような慣用表現には the が付く。

in the morning / in the afternoon / in the evening / in the daytime

## 9. 同じ語が繰り返される場合

同じ語が繰り返される慣用表現には冠詞は付かない。

arm in arm / face to face / day by day / hand in hand / side by side / from morning to night

## 10. 「人間」を表す名詞と冠詞

「人間」を表す名詞 man には冠詞は付けない。

man が複数形で「人間」を表す場合もある。また，「人間」を humans や human being とも表せるが，後者は他の動物や神との対比をする場合に用いられる。

## 練習問題

Ⅰ. 次の (　) 内に適当な冠詞を入れなさい。

1. Turning to (　　) right, you will find (　　) house you want.
2. Many man has made (　　) same mistake.
3. He is (　　) right man in (　　) right place.
4. At that time I met him in (　　) morning.
5. She patted me gently on (　　) shoulder.

II．次の各文の誤りを訂正しなさい。
1．Are you going to Tokyo by the car?
2．He works hard the night and day.
3．Have you eaten a dinner yet?
4．If you commit a crime, you will be sent to a prison.
5．Suddenly I came the face to the face with Professor Jones.

III．日本語に合うように（　　）内に適切な英語を入れなさい。
1．その兄弟は同じ長所と短所を持っている。
　　The brothers have the same (　　) and the same (　　).
2．東京からロンドンまで飛行機でどのくらいお金がかかりますか。
　　How much does it (　　) to go from Tokyo to London (　　) plane?
3．人間は好きな時にいつでも新しい文を作ることができる。
　　Humans can produce novel sentences (　　) they want to.
4．ここが彼がかつて通訳として働いていた会社です。
　　This is the company where he (　　) worked as an (　　).
5．彼は日中は眠り夜に起きて執筆に取りかかることにしている。
　　He makes it a (　　) to sleep in the daytime and wake up at night to set (　　) writing.

IV．次の日本語を英語にしなさい。
1．誰かが私に近づいてきて私の肩をぽんと叩いた。
2．彼らは腕をくんで怒鳴りながらやってきた。
3．彼らのうちの何人かに賄賂が贈られたという噂があったが，彼はニューヨークの市長に選ばれた。
4．もし罪を犯したら刑務所に入れられますよ。
5．その学生は2人ともゼミを休んだので，彼らの指導教官は何をしてよいやら途方に暮れてしまった。

# Chapter 6　冠　　詞(3)

## 1. 定冠詞 the が付く固有名詞
固有名詞には通常冠詞を付けないが，次のような名詞には the を付ける。
① 河川や海洋の名前

the Avon / the Amazon / the Pacific Ocean / the Atlantic Ocean
② 群島

the Bahamas / the Hebrides / the Marshal Islands / the Shetlands
③ 山脈

the Alps / the Andes / the Himalayas / the Rockies
④ 運河

the Panama Canal / the Suez Canal
⑤ 海峡，湾，岬

the English Channel / the Gulf of Mexico / the Cape of Good Hope /
⑥ 公共の建築物や施設（ホテル，レストラン，劇場，映画館，博物館，図書館，病院等）

the Imperial Hotel / the Globe Theater / the British Museum / the Bodleian Library / the Red Cross Hospital
⑦ 乗り物

the Mayflower / the Victory
⑧ 新聞，雑誌，書物

The New York Times / The Observer / the Bible

## 2. 冠詞が付かない名詞
冠詞を付けない名詞には次のようなものがある。

① 曜日や月を表す名詞

Sunday / Monday / January / February

② 大陸の名前

Australia / Europe / Africa / Asia

③ 町の名前

New York / Rome / London

④ 湖

Lake Michigan / Lake Biwa / Loch Ness

⑤ 山の名前

Mount Everest / Snowdon / Vesuvius

⑥ 公園，駅，橋，大学，寺院，通り等

Ueno Park / Tokyo Station / London Bridge / Kyushu University / Westminster Abby / Oxford Street

⑦ 建物などの名詞がその本来の機能を表す場合

I go to school every day.

He was sent to prison.

He went to hospital.

## 3．国名形容詞に the が付く場合

国名形容詞に the を付けるとその国民を表す。

the English / the Japanese / the Germans

## 4．計量・数量の単位と定冠詞

計量・数量の単位を表すときは the を付ける。

by the hour / by the dozen

## 5．the ＋単数名詞

the ＋単数名詞で「～というもの」という種類全体を表す。

The tiger is a dangerous animal.
The horse is a domestic animal.

## 6．楽器を表す名詞

楽器を表す名詞には the が付く。

I play the guitar / the cello / the piano.

## 7．the ＋形容詞

the ＋形容詞で「～の人々」をいう意味を表すことがある。

the young（若者たち）　　the old（老人たち）　　the poor（貧乏人）
the rich（金持ち）　　the brave（勇者たち）

## 8．定冠詞と場所を表す慣用表現

特定の名詞に the を付けると場所を表す慣用表現ができる。

in the dark（暗闇の中）　　in the distance（遠くへ）　　in the shade（日陰で）　　in the light（明るみで）

## 9．「～として」という意味の as の後の名詞

「～として」という意味の as の後の名詞には冠詞は付けないことがある。

He played a role as Master of Ceremonies.

## 10．「第二次世界大戦」に冠詞はつけるか

「第二次世界大戦」と言う場合 the を付ける場合と付けない場合がある。

the Second World War
World War Ⅱ

## 練習問題

Ⅰ．次の（　）内に適当な冠詞を入れなさい。ただし，冠詞を入れる必要のない場合は×を入れなさい。
1．We booked a room at (　　) Imperial Hotel.
2．He sides with (　　) weak and crushes (　　) strong.
3．He is going to act as (　　) chairman of the committee.
4．He played (　　) cello at the concert hall.
5．We met him at (　　) Tokyo Station last night.

Ⅱ．次の各文の誤りを訂正しなさい。
1．I met him by chance at British Museum.
2．Last Sunday, we went to school to play baseball.
3．We hired the boat by an hour.
4．She lives near the Lake Biwa.
5．We sat in a shade of a beach umbrella.

Ⅲ．日本語に合うように（　　）内に適切な英語を入れなさい。
1．上野公園は今桜が満開なので，すぐ見に行きませんか。
　 The cherry-trees in Ueno Park are full in (　　), so why don't we go to see them at (　　)?
2．鉛筆は1ダース単位で売られます。
　 Pencils are sold by the (　　).
3．第二次世界大戦では多くの死傷者が出ました。
　 World War Ⅱ sustained heavy (　　).
4．若者達は老人達の言うことを誤解しがちである。
　 The young are (　　) to misunderstand (　　) the old say.

5．帝国ホテルに一部屋予約したいのですが。

 I would like to (　　) a room at the Imperial Hotel.

Ⅳ．次の日本語を英語にしなさい。
1．彼は左足が不自由でしたが，富士山に登ろうとした。
2．オックスフォード通りに沿って数分歩いて行けば，右手にその図書館が見えてきます。
3．私たちは3時間も車を走らせて，やっと遠くに人家が一軒見えました。
4．彼は先日病院へ行き医者に骨折の治療をしてもらった。
5．日本人が平和を愛好する国民であるあることは言うまでもないことである。

# Chapter 7　動　　詞(1)

## 1．時や条件を表す節での注意点

when, after, before, until, if など時や条件を表す接続詞で形成される節には，未来のことを表すことがあっても単純未来を表す will は用いず，動詞は現在時制で表す。

　　When I graduate from the university, I will marry her.

■ただし疑問文に疑問詞 when や if が使われる場合 will が使える。

　　When will the letter be here?

　　I wonder if he will come home tomorrow.

## 2．動作や習慣を表す場合

繰り返し行われる動作や習慣を表す場合，動詞は進行形ではなく現在形になる。

　　I play tennis everyday.

　　I take medicine after dinner.

## 3．過去の出来事の列挙

ある出来事が過去のある時点より前に起こった場合は過去完了形 had ＋過去分詞で表すが，過去の出来事を起こった順に述べる時にはそれぞれ過去形で表す。

　　Last year I went to London and bought a lot of souvenir at Harrods.

## 4．「～するようになる」という意味の動詞

「～するようになる」という場合 begin を使い，名詞や形容詞が伴う場合は

become を使う。

　　I begin to feel tired.

　　He became sick.

「～するようになる」を表す表現は他に come to ＋動詞の原形があるが，この場合 come to の後には know, realize, love, hate, like など状態を表す動詞がくる。また，learn to ＋動詞の原形も「～するようになる」の意味を持つが，これは経験などを積んで「～するようになる」という含みがある。

## 5．「結婚する」という意味の動詞

「結婚する」という意味の marry や get married は後ろに with を用いない。

　　He married me.　×  He married with me.

　　She got married to a Frenchman.

## 6．enjoy は目的語をとる

enjoy は他動詞であるため必ず後ろに目的語がくる。

　○ I enjoyed myself at the party.

　○ I enjoyed the party.

　× I enjoyed at the party.

目的語に動名詞がくる場合もある。

　　I enjoy playing tennis.

■ enter や discuss も他動詞であるため注意を要する。

　○ I entered the room.

　× I entered into the room.

　○ We discussed the problem

　× We discussed about the problem.

■ こうした動詞には他に leave, reach, inhabit, attend などがある。また，日本語では他動詞と考えられる動詞が英語では自動詞となる動詞としては，

listen, add, account, complain, agree などがある。

## 7．「～を着る」という動詞の注意点

「～を着る」という表現に関して put on と wear を混同することがあるが，put on は着るという動作を表し，wear は着ている状態を表す。

 He is wearing a red shirt.
 I will hold your bag while you put on your coat.

## 8．「～を教える」という動詞の注意点

「～を教える」に関して学問や知識を教える場合は teach を使い，住所，場所，方向など単なる情報を教える場合は tell を使う。

 I taught the students English.
 Could you tell me the way to the station?

## 9．「～を見る」という動詞の注意点

「～を見る」には様々な表現が可能であるが，動いたり変化するものを見る場合は watch を使い，動かないものを凝視する場合は look at を，あるものが目に入ってくる場合 see を使う。

 He watched her go out of the room.
 I looked at stars through a telescope.
 I have never seen such a big dog.
 ■ただし映画などを見たり野球などを観戦する場合は see を用いることがある。
 I was seeing a baseball game on TV.

## 10．「～を借りる」という動詞の注意点

「～を借りる」という表現に関して，お金を払って物を借りる場合は rent を，お金を払わないで物を借りる場合は borrow を使う。

I rented a car for a week.

Can I borrow these books for a week?

■ lend は貸すという意味があるが，無料で貸す場合に用いられる。


## 練習問題

Ⅰ．次の各文の（　）内から正しい語を選びなさい。

1．I (put on, wore ) a black suit at the funeral.
2．Please (tell, teach) me your phone number.
3．I (became, came ) to like studying English.
4．He enjoys (looking at, watching) TV when he has time.
5．It costs a lot of money to (borrow, rent) a wedding dress.

Ⅱ．次の各文の誤りを訂正しなさい。

1．If I will find your watch, I will send it to you by post.
2．He has once climbed the mountain some five years ago.
3．He got married with a French woman three years ago.
4．A man from China entered into the room with a white coat on.
5．I became to feel like throwing up because of seasickness.

Ⅲ．日本語に合うように（　　）内に適切な英語を入れなさい。

1．私は一日おきにこの薬を飲みます。

　　I (　　) this medicine every (　　) day.

2．彼がヨーロッパの旅行から帰って来たら空港に出迎えに行くつもりです。

　　When he comes back (　　) his European trip, I'll be (　　) the airport to meet him.

3．青いシャツを着ている選手の巧みな動作が私の目を引いた。
　　The fine motion of the player (　　) a blue shirt (　　) my eye.
4．私は最近物忘れが激しくなっているので何でもメモを取っておかないといけない。
　　Recently I have become so (　　) that I have to (　　) a note of everything.
5．彼女は大学を卒業したらアメリカ人と結婚する予定だそうです。
　　She plans to (　　) an American after she graduates (　　) the university.

Ⅳ．次の日本語を英語にしなさい。
1．あなたの電話番号を教えて下さい。折り返し電話いたします。
2．給料日まで1万円貸してくれませんか。
3．私たちはその会議に出席し来年度の賃上げを要求した。
4．私は以前は早起きして朝食前に1時間ほど散歩したものだった。
5．私はへたですが野球が大好きで，日曜日には雨が降らなければ3時間くらいやることにしています。

# Chapter 8　動　　詞(2)

## 1. 「わかっている」という動詞の注意点

「わかっている」という表現に関して，既にわかっている場合には know を，知らなかったことがわかるようになる場合 realize を，あることを学んでわかるようになる場合 learn を，探査などで知らなかったことがわかる場合 discover を使う。

　　He knew that she was still alive.
　　I didn't realize how late it was.
　　I learned many things from this book.
　　The astronaut discovered that the planet had no water.

## 2. 「似ている」という動詞の注意点

「似ている」という意味の動詞 resemble は他動詞であり，目的語を後ろに従える。日本語で判断すると「～に似ている」となるので，resemble の後に to を従えそうであるがそうではない。

　○ You don't resemble your mother.
　× You don't resemble to your mother.

## 3. 「勝つ」という動詞の注意点

試合などで人やチームに勝つ場合は beat を，試合に勝つ場合は win を使う。

　　We always beat the team at baseball.
　　Our team won the game over a seeded team.

## 4．「選ぶ」という動詞の注意点

「選ぶ」という表現に関しては choose, elect, select などがあるが，2人または2つ以上のものから選ぶ時は choose，3人または3つ以上のものから選ぶ場合は select，選挙などで選ぶ場合は elect を使う。

## 5．「調べる」という動詞の注意点

「調べる」という表現に関して単語，電話番号，時刻などを調べる場合は look up，性質や病状を調べる場合は examine，より綿密な調査をする場合は inspect または investigate，分析して調べる場合は analyze，研究や調査で未知の事実を調べる場合は find を使う。

　　I looked up a strange word in a dictionary.
　　The mechanic investigated the tires.
　　The police are analyzing his motive.
　　I found the answer to the question.

## 6．「負傷する」という動詞の注意点

「負傷する」という表現に関して，交通事故などで負傷する場合 be injured または be hurt を，戦争などで負傷する場合は be wounded を使う。

　　I had my arm injured in the traffic accident.
　　I had my arm wounded in the war.

## 7．「～が開かれる」という動詞の注意点

「～が開かれる」という表現に関して，会議や催し物が開かれる場合は open ではなく hold の過去分詞形を使う。

　　The next meeting will be held on May 17.
　　■ただし以下のような文では open は「始まる」という意味を持つ。
The meeting opened yesterday.

## 8. 「覚える」という動詞の注意点

「覚える」という表現に関して，何かを覚えている場合またはそれを思い出す場合は remember を，意識して暗記したり覚えたりする場合は memorize または learn by heart を使う。

　　I remember that I posted your letter.

　　I memorize ten English words every day.

## 9. 現在完了と時を表す表現

現在完了は時制は現在であるため明らかに過去を表す語句，例えば just now, 〜ago, yesterday, the other day などとともに用いることはできない。また，疑問詞の when とともに用いることもできない。

　　× The game has started just now.

　　○ The game started just now.

　　× When has he returned home from a trip to London?

　　○ When did he return home from a trip to London?

　　■ただし today, this morning, this year, lately, recently などの現在時を含む語句は現在完了形とともに用いることが可能である。

## 10. 進行形にできない動詞

動詞の中には進行形にできないものがある。

① 状態を表す動詞

resemble, seem, belong, contain, remember, forget など

　　○ She resembles her mother.

　　× She is resembling her mother.

② 感情を表す動詞

like, hate, love, fear, praise など

　　○ She likes her father.

　　× She is liking her father.

③　知識を表す動詞

know, believe, think, realize, understand など

○ I understand the word.

× I'm understanding the word.

■ただし少しずつ変化している状態や，一時的状態が繰り返されている場合などは例外的に進行形になることがある。

He is resembling his father more and more as time goes by.

I am understanding Greek little by little.

## 11.「許す」という動詞の注意点

「許す」という表現に関して，ある行動をすることを許す場合は permit，罪を許す場合は forgive，入会や入学など人が入ることを許す場合 admit を使う。

My father permitted me to go abroad.

He forgave me for breaking my promise.

He was admitted to this college.

## 練習問題

Ⅰ．次の各文の（　）内から正しい語を選びなさい。

1．I wanted to go on a trip with my friend, but my parents didn't (admit, permit) me.
2．Many companies (have gone, went) bankrupt recently.
3．I have just (memorized, remembered) how to operate this machine.
4．The president has (chosen, elected) Mr. Smith as his successor.
5．The meeting, which (opened, was held) yesterday, will end next week.

Ⅱ．次の各文の誤りを訂正しなさい。
1. He resembles to his father, doesn't he?
2. I had gone to Tokyo last week.
3. I investigated his phone number in a telephone book.
4. He was injured his right leg in the traffic accident.
5. Our team won the other team in the baseball game.

Ⅲ．日本語に合うように（　　　）内に適切な英語を入れなさい。
1. 彼は南北戦争で左足を負傷した。
   He had his left leg (　　　) in the Civil War.
2. 彼は気のおけないやつなので嘘をついても許してしまうのです。
   He is a great guy to be with, so I forgive him for (　　　) a lie.
3. 次の学会はいつどこで開かれるのですか。
   When and where is the next conference to be (　　　)?
4. 私は突然会議に提出しなければならない書類に目を通さなければならないことを思い出した。
   I suddenly remembered that I had to look (　　　) a document to (　　　) to the meeting.
5. その双子はとてもよく似ているので見分けがつきません。
   The twins (　　　) each other so closely that we cannot tell one from the (　　　).

Ⅳ．次の日本語を英語にしなさい。
1. 彼は何百人もの応募者の中からその賞に選ばれた。
2. 私は駅へ着いた時，財布がなくなっていることに気が付いた。
3. 彼は英語の授業を4回さぼったため単位が取れなかった。
4. 駅へ着いた時，終電は既に出た後でした。
5. 長い間彼から何の連絡もありません。どうしているのでしょう。

# Chapter 9　形容詞

## 1．人の感情を表す表現の注意点

人の感情を表す表現には受動態になるものが多く，excited, bored, interested, moved, impressed, tired, worried, frightened など過去分詞形になる。

　　○ I was very excited at that time.
　　× I was very exciting at that time.

現在分詞の形は色々な感情を引き起こさせる場合に用いられるので注意を要す。

　　The TV program is very moving.
　　The baseball game was very exciting.

## 2．「安い」という表現の注意点

物が安いという場合は cheap を使い，値段が安いという場合は low を使う。逆に物が高いという場合は expensive，値段が高いという場合は high を使う。

　　○ The bag is cheap.
　　× The bag is low.
　　○ The price of the bag is low.
　　○ The bag is expensive.

## 3．「広い」という表現の注意点

幅が広い場合は wide，狭い場合は narrow を使い，大きさや面積が広い場合は big, large を使い，面積が狭い場合は small を使う。

○ Africa is very big.
× Africa is very wide.
○ The street is wide.
○ Japan is a small country.

## 4．very の使い方

　like, love, respect, thank you などの後に very much を置くことはあるが，形容詞や副詞の後に付けることはなく，それらを強調する場合 very を前に付ける。
　○ I was very angry.
　× I was angry very much.

## 5．「そんな〜」という表現の語順

　形容詞＋名詞で「そんな〜」という意味を表す場合，such (a) 形容詞＋名詞となる。形容詞だけの場合 so をその前に置く。また，so ＋形容詞＋(a)＋名詞という形もあるが日常の会話などでは使われない。
　○ I have never seen such a stupid man.
　× I have never seen a so stupid man.
　○ He is so stupid.

## 6．「恥ずかしい」という表現の注意点

　人の前で恥をかくなどして恥ずかしいと思う場合 ashamed ではなく embarrassed を使う。
　○ I felt embarrassed when I made a false step.
　× I felt ashamed when I made a false step.

## 7．「遅れている」という表現の注意点

　「遅れている」という場合，時計などが遅れている場合は slow，人が仕事

などに遅れる，また交通機関などが遅れている場合は late を使う。

○ My watch is slow.

× My watch is late.

○ I'm sorry I'm late.

## 8．「はやい」という表現の注意点

「はやい」に関して，時期，時刻が早い場合は early，速度が速い場合は fast を使う。

○ TGV is a very fast train.

× TGV is a very early train.

## 9．物の高さを表す表現の注意点

物の高さを表す場合は high，人の背丈や木などの高さを表す場合は tall を使う。

○ How tall are you?

× How high are you?

## 10．極端な性質を表す形容詞の注意点

極端な性質を表す形容詞にはそれ以上強めることはできないため，通常 very を付けない。

○ The food was terrible.

× The food was very terrible.

こうした形容詞には awful, excellent, marvelous, enormous, huge, tiny, astonished, amazed, delighted, miserable などがある。

## 練習問題

Ⅰ．次の各文の誤りを訂正しなさい。
1．You should gain as many knowledge as possible.
2．The number of the people here is much fewer than we expected.
3．She has less books than I have.
4．There was a very enormous traffic jam in the downtown.
5．The car I bought yesterday is very high.

Ⅱ．次の各文の（　　）内から正しい語を選びなさい。
1．Three (hundreds, hundred) teachers took part in the conference.
2．You should take (a few, a little) more care with your work.
3．I met many (interested, interesting) people at the party.
4．Hurry up, or you will be (slow, late) for the meeting.
5．He took a picture of (so, such) a tall foreigner.

Ⅲ．日本語に合うように（　　）内に適切な英語を入れなさい。
1．その電車は3分早く出た。
　　The train (　　) three minutes (　　).
2．数秒のところで電車に乗り遅れたので会議に30分遅刻しました。
　　I was thirty minutes (　　) to the meeting because I missed the train by (　　).
3．彼はよい知らせを聞いて大変喜んだ。
　　He was really (　　) to hear the good news.
4．「その鞄高かったんでしょう。」「そうでもないですよ。本当はセールで買ったんです。」
　　"That bag must have been very (　　)." "It wasn't. In fact, I bought it

(    ) a sale."
5．その時はあまり時間がなかったので，私たちはタクシーで駅へ行った。
   We didn't have (    ) time then, so we went to the station (    ) taxi.

## Ⅳ．次の日本語を英語にしなさい。

1．議論の時間がほとんどないのではないかと心配です。
2．今年の6月は晴れた日がほとんどなかった。
3．その外国人は非常に早口でしゃべったので彼の言うことが分かるものがほとんどいなかった。
4．あそこの狭い道を南に行くと駅に行けます。
5．彼らは初めて海外旅行をするというのでうきうきしていた。

# Chapter 10　副　詞

1．副詞が修飾するもの

　副詞は主に動詞，形容詞，他の副詞を修飾するが，場合によっては名詞，代名詞，句，節，文を修飾することがある。

　① 動詞の場合

　　His book accurately reflects scientific thinking of the time.

　② 形容詞の場合

　　I feel rather sick.

　③ 副詞の場合

　　He was speaking very slowly.

　④ 名詞，代名詞の場合

　　I like fruits, especially ripe ones.

　　Only you did it.

　⑤ 句の場合

　　He studies late into the night.

　⑥ 節の場合

　　I feel sluggish probably because it is raining.

　⑦ 文の場合

　　Obviously she is in the wrong.


2．副詞の位置

　① 形容詞，副詞，句，節を修飾する場合は上記のようにその直前に置く。

　② 動詞の場合

　　●方法，状態を表す副詞は通常動詞の後に置く。目的語や補語があればそ

の後に置く。

受動態の場合は過去分詞の前後に置かれる。

Everyone left slowly.

John worded the letter carefully.

I was strictly brought up. / I was brought up strictly.

● 回数や否定を表す副詞は動詞の前に置かれるが，be 動詞や助動詞があればその後に置く。

He always comes late for school.

He is always short of money.

I could hardly sleep last night.

I have almost finished my homework.

③　場所，時，方法，状態を表す副詞の位置

　時を表す副詞は文頭に置かれる場合もあるが，文尾に置くのが普通である。場所を表す副詞と時を表す副詞がある場合，場所を表す副詞を前に置く。また，方法，状態を表す副詞が加わる場合，場所を表す副詞，方法，状態を表す副詞，時を表す副詞の順になる。

He recited the poem perfectly yesterday.

He answered the question here foolishly yesterday.

④　文全体を修飾する副詞は文頭または動詞の前に置かれる。

Evidently John lost his mind.

John evidently lost his mind.

こうした副詞に以下のようなものがある。

fortunately, luckily, happily, surprisingly, regrettably, unfortunately, probably, possibly, certainly, surely, evidently, honestly, seriously, strictly, truthfully など

## 3．文全体を修飾する副詞

副詞の中には文全体を修飾する副詞のように文頭に置かれて主語に対する

価値判断を表すものがある。

　　Wisely, he didn't accept the offer.

　　Rightly, he left the proposal concrete.

　こうした副詞には以下のようなものがある。

　correctly, incorrectly, falsely, wrongly, unwisely, cleverly, intelligently, foolishly, stupidly, reasonably など


## 4．価値判断を表す副詞

　文頭に置いて主語に対する価値判断を表す副詞の中には，文尾に置かれると様態を表す場合がある。

　　He answered the questions foolishly.（彼はその問題に愚かな答え方をした）


## 5．様態や方法を表す副詞

　様態や方法を表す副詞は，文尾に置かれる場合と動詞の前に置かれる場合とで意味が異なる場合がある。

　　He analyzed the material microscopically.（彼はその素材を顕微鏡で分析した）

　　He microscopically analyzed the material.（彼はその素材を詳細に分析した）


## 6．否定を表す語と副詞

　副詞の中には否定を表す語の前に生じる場合と後ろに生じる場合とで意味が変わることがある。

　　a．I particularly don't want to see the game.

　　b．I don't particularly want to see the game.

　aの文はその試合を見たくないという気持ちが強いが，bの文ではその試合を見てもよいが特に見たいとは思わないという意味がある。

## 7．句を修飾する副詞

very は形容詞，副詞を修飾するが，句を修飾できるのは much である。

○ They are much about an age.（彼らはほぼ同年齢だ）

× They are very about an age.

## 8．比較級や最上級の修飾

very も much も最上級を修飾できるが，それぞれ語順が変わるので注意を要する。また，比較級を修飾するのは much の方である。

He is the very tallest man in this class.

He is much the tallest man in this class.

He is much taller than you.

## 9．副詞 enough の注意点

enough は形容詞，副詞の直後に置かれ，後ろに不定詞節を伴うことがある。

○ He was kind enough to take me to the station.

× He was enough kind to take me to the station.

## 10．時を表す副詞 just now の注意点

時を表す副詞 just now は現在時制と過去時制の文に用いられる。

The plane is landing just now.

He went out just now.（彼はたった今外出しました）

## 11．「〜もまた」という表現の注意点

「〜もまた」という意味の too は肯定文に，either は否定文に用いられる。

He is ready. I am, too.

He can't drive a car. I can't, either.

## 練習問題

Ⅰ．次の各文の誤りを訂正しなさい。
1．My father is very taller than I am.
2．If he doesn't go skating, I will not go, too.
3．He is very the best student in this class.
4．He has just now done his homework.
5．My father takes a walk before breakfast usually.

Ⅱ．次の各文の（　　）内から正しい語を選びなさい。
1．The man from England spoke English slowly (much, enough)
2．The teacher has not turned up (already, yet).
3．It has been raining (heavy, heavily) since last night.
4．She tried (hard, hardly) to open the box.
5．I was able to pronounce the sentence (precise, precisely).

Ⅲ．日本語に合うように（　　）内に適切な英語を入れなさい。
1．彼は大胆にも彼女の面前で彼女の悪口を言った。
　　He was bold (　　) to speak (　　) of her in her presence.
2．彼は大変興奮したのでその夜眠れなかった。
　　He was too much (　　) to sleep that night.
3．彼の長話にはまったくうんざりです。
　　I'm very (　　) of his long talk.
4．彼は簡単に殺されかねなかった。
　　He could have (　　) been killed.
5．彼女が適任者であることは明らかである。
　　She is evidently the (　　) person in the (　　) place.

Ⅳ．次の日本語を英語にしなさい。
1．率直に言ってあなたはそれを心配する必要はないと思います。
2．君が行かないなら私も行かない。
3．私の故郷はほとんど見違えるほど変わっていました。
4．私はこの 20 年間風邪一つ引いたことがありません。
5．彼はその男の人がただ貧しい服装をしているという理由だけでその人を軽蔑します。

# Chapter 11　前　置　詞

## 1．時を表す前置詞 at の注意点

at は時刻，比較的短い時間，年齢を表す場合に用いられる。

at seven o'clock, at night, at the age of fifteen, at Christmas, at the New Year, at present, at the beginning of this year, at that time

## 2．時を表す前置詞 in の注意点

in は月，季節，年代，世紀，時代など比較的長い期間を表す場合や，日にち，曜日に限定されない朝・昼・夜を表す名詞に用いられる。

in October, in summer, in 1990, in the twentieth century, in our scientific age, in one's childhood, in the morning, in the afternoon, in the evening

## 3．時を表す前置詞 on の注意点

on は曜日，特定の日や時を表す場合に用いられる。特に morning, afternoon, evening, night などに修飾語が付いている場合には on が用いられる。

on Sunday, on the fifth of June, on New Year's day, on a fine morning, on Sunday afternoon, on Friday night

## 4．時を表す名詞の前の前置詞が省略される場合

時を表す名詞の前に this, next, last などがあるときはその前に前置詞は付けない。

I'm going to Tokyo next week.

I'm going to the party this evening.

I was busy last month.

## 5．前置詞 during の注意点

during は前置詞であるためその後に節を続けることはできない。節を続ける場合は while を用いる。

The man was sleeping during her absence.

The man was sleeping while she was absent.

## 6．時を表す前置詞 for の注意点

「～の間」という期間を表す for は継続を表す動詞とともに用いられ，その後ろには数詞が続く。

○ He stayed there for ten days.

× He stayed there during ten days.

## 7．「～たてば」という意味の前置詞 in の注意点

「～たてば」という時間の経過を表す in は現在を起点とする時間の経過を表すため，「～後に」という after と区別される。

○ He will get well in a few days.

× He will get well after a few days.

## 8．「～までに」という意味を表す前置詞 by の注意点

「～までに」という意味を表す by は完了を表す動詞とともに用いられ，動作や状態の継続を表す till (until) と区別される。

○ He will finish the work by tomorrow.

× He will finish the work till tomorrow.

○ He will stay here till tomorrow.

## 9. 場所を表す前置詞 at の注意点

場所を表す at は比較的狭い場所を表し，in は国，地方，町，島など広い場所を表す。

He spent five days in Tokyo.

He arrived at the station in Tokyo.

He arrived in London.

広い狭いといった尺度で示せない地点については at を用いる。

He is standing at the corner of the street

## 10. 前置詞 by と with の違い

物や道具を使ってという「～で」という場合，前置詞は by ではなく with を使う。

He cut the tree with his hatchet.

by は行為者，方法，手段を表すため次のように用いる。

The tree was cut by him.

He passed the examination by studying hard.

He went there by train.

The city was destroyed by the earthquake.


## 練習問題

Ⅰ．次の各文の（　）内に適当な前置詞を入れなさい。

1．He ate candy (　　　) his work.
2．I agree (　　　) your proposal.
3．He made a speech (　　　) English.
4．He shot a bird (　　　) the air gun which he bought yesterday.
5．We had our picture taken (　　　) the corner of the street.

Ⅱ．次の各文の誤りを訂正しなさい。
1．He called on the teacher for the summer vacation.
2．The second term begins from September.
3．The woman danced at the playing of the band till late in night.
4．The sun went down, but it remained light during about half an hour.
5．The train for Tokyo will start from this track for ten minutes.

Ⅲ．日本語に合うように（　　　）内に適切な英語を入れなさい。
1．その建物は今月末までにできあがるでしょう。
　　The building will be (　　) (　　) the end of this month.
2．私はジョーンズさんとニューヨーク滞在中に友達になりました。
　　I (　　) friends with Jones (　　) my stay in New York.
3．その島へは船で行かれるのですかそれとも飛行機ですか。
　　Are you going to the island (　　) ship or (　　) plane？
4．その電車は定刻には来ませんでした。
　　The train didn't come (　　) time.
5．彼は1990年10月5日の朝，自分の自宅で亡くなりました。
　　He died at his house (　　) the morning of October 5, 1990.

Ⅳ．次の日本語を英語にしなさい。
1．私の家はその駅から歩いてわずかのところにあります。
2．報道によるとその交通事故で20人の人が重傷を負ったそうです。
3．彼は突然その壁の後ろから出てきました。
4．私は風邪のため5日も学校を休みました。
5．日曜日の午後3時ごろ再びここへきて頂けませんでしょうか。

# Chapter 12　関係代名詞

## 1．非制限用法を持つ関係代名詞
　who, which, that といった関係代名詞で非制限用法を持つのは who と which だけである。
　　○ He has three sons, who are doctors.
　　○ He solved the problem, which I thought was very difficult.
　　× He solved the problem, that I thought was very difficult.

## 2．非制限用法を持つ関係副詞
　when, where, why といった関係副詞で非制限用法を持つのは when と where だけである。
　　○ He was born in 1945, when the Pacific War ended.
　　○ I went to London, where my brother lives.
　　○ There is no reason why he should be here all by himself.
　　× There is no reason, why he should be here all by himself.

## 3．性質や地位などを表すものが先行詞の場合
　先行詞が人を表しても，それが関係代名詞節内で性質や地位などを表す場合 who ではなく which や that を用いる場合がある。
　　He is not the bad guy that he was five years ago.
　　He is an accountant supervisor, which his brother is not.

## 4．「～する人たち」という表現と関係代名詞
　関係代名詞の who が those と結びついて those who となり，「～する人た

ち」という意味を持つ場合がある。

 Heaven helps those who help themselves.

## 5．非制限用法の which がさすもの

 非制限用法の which が前の文，節，句を指す場合がある。

 Children ran about the room for a long time, which kept her awake.

 He tried to solve the problem, which was found to be impossible.

## 6．関係代名詞が that になる場合

 先行詞に最上級や序数詞が付いたり，only，every，all，any，no，the very，much，little などの語が付いている場合，関係代名詞は that になることが多い。

 This is one of the best products that the company has.

 He wants everything that he sees in the store.

 He spent all the money that he had.

 ■先行詞が人と物（または動物）の両方である場合，関係代名詞は that になる。

 The car ran over a man and his dog that were just crossing the road.

## 7．関係代名詞 what の注意点

 関係代名詞の which や that は先行詞を必ず必要とするが，関係代名詞の what はその中に先行詞が含まれ，「〜すること」，「〜するもの」といった意味を持つ。

 Don't put off till tomorrow what you can do today.

 What you have to do is to study hard.

 ■ Don't put off till tomorrow that you can do today. のようには言わないので注意。

## 8. 関係形容詞 what の注意点

what が関係形容詞（whose も関係形容詞）として用いられ、「～するすべての」といった意味を表すことがある。また、little, few, small などを what の次に置いて「少ないながら～するすべての」といった意味を表すこともある。

　　Lend me what money you have.
　　I gave him what little money I had.

## 9. その他の関係代名詞

as, but, than が関係代名詞の働きをもつことがある。

　　I want the same car as you have.
　　He had completely misjudged the situation, as we discovered later.
　　He goes to school on foot, as is usual with him.
　　There is no rule but has some exceptions.
　　We have more apples than we could eat in a day.

## 10. 関係副詞の how は先行詞を持たない

関係副詞の how は先行詞なしで用いられ、the way how といった表現は使われない。先行詞と考えられる way を用いる場合は the way (that) または the way in which という形になる。また、how か way を省略した That is how～ または That is the way という形は可能である。

　　The best way (that) you can speak English is to speak with native speakers.
　　That is how I solved the problem.
　　That is the way I solved the problem.

## 練習問題

Ⅰ．次の2つの文を関係詞を用いて1つの文にしなさい。
1. His father has three sons. He is the youngest of them.
2. I left my coat. I cannot remember the place.
3. I have done it. You told me to do it.
4. My father slipped on the ice. We all laughed at it.
5. Why did the teacher arrive late? The boy asked the reason.

Ⅱ．次の（　）内に適当な関係詞を入れなさい。
1. I spoke to a man (　　) I thought to be my uncle.
2. My father has forgotten (　　) he promised.
3. He spends (　　) money he earns on his hobby.
4. This is the house in (　　) I lived in my childhood.
5. You should choose such books (　　) make you better.
6. He told me (　　) this computer works.
7. Sunday is the day (　　) my father goes to sports center.
8. This is one of the most important things (　　) you should do soon.
9. He says he caught a cold, (　　) is a lie.
10. He ate the same foods (　　) we did.

Ⅲ．日本語に合うように（　）内に適切な英語を入れなさい。
1. 私を助けてくれることのできる人は世界中で彼だけです。
   He is the only (　　) in the world (　　) can help me.
2. それは彼がまだ見たことのないような絵だった。
   It was (　　) a picture (　　) he had never seen.
3. 彼は正しいと思うことをすぐに実行します。

He does soon (　　) he thinks is right.
4．彼は私を医者だと思ったのだが，これには驚いた。
He thought I was a doctor, (　　) surprised me.
5．私の故郷は 10 年ほど前に住んでいたころとほとんど変わっていません。
My hometown is almost the same (　　) it was some ten years ago when I lived there.

Ⅳ．次の日本語を英語にしなさい。
1．もっと忙しくない時にまた出直して来ましょう。
2．例外のない規則はほとんどない。
3．彼は勤勉だったが，彼の兄は決してそうではなかった。
4．彼の私たちへの口の利き方は疑い深げだった。
5．私はその戦争については新聞で読んでいる以上のことは何も知りません。

# Chapter 13　準 動 詞

1．動詞の目的語が不定詞の場合と動名詞の場合

　動詞が目的語に不定詞をとる場合と動名詞をとる場合とで意味が異なることがある。これは不定詞はある時点を起点にこれから起こることを表すが，動名詞は事実を表すことができるためである。

　　I must remember to lock the door.（私は忘れずにドアに鍵をかけなければならない）

　　I remember locking the door.（私はドアに鍵をかけたことを覚えている）

　　I forgot to see him.（私は彼に会うのを忘れた）

　　I forgot seeing him.（私は彼に会ったことを忘れた）

　　I regret to tell you.（私はあなたに話さなければならないのが残念だ）

　　I regret telling you.（私はあなたに話したことを後悔している）

　　He tried to solve the problem.（彼はその問題を解こうとした）

　　He tried solving the problem.（彼は試しにその問題を解いてみた）

　　He stopped to talk.（彼は話すために立ち止まった）

　　He stopped talking.（彼は話すのをやめた）

2．不定詞を目的語にとる動詞

　動詞の中には動名詞ではなく不定詞を目的語にとる動詞がある。

　　I wish to see the manager.

　　I have desired to marry her.

　こうした動詞に afford, care, contrive, mean, expect, learn, agree, pretend, decide, choose, refuse, hesitate, seek, plan などがある。

## 3．動名詞を目的語にとる動詞

動詞の中には不定詞ではなく動名詞を目的語にとる動詞がある。

He finished writing a letter to her.

Do you mind opening the window?

こうした動詞に advise, enjoy, avoid, admit, miss, deny, resist, repeat, stand, give up, go on, put off などがある。

## 4．分詞の位置

分詞が一語の場合は名詞の直前に置かれるが，他の修飾語をともなって長くなる場合は名詞の後ろに置かれる。

Look at the sleeping baby.

Look at the baby sleeping on the sofa.

Look at the broken vase.

Look at the vase broken into pieces.

## 5．知覚動詞の注意点

知覚動詞などがとる目的語の後に現在分詞がくる場合と動詞の原形がくる場合とでは意味が異なる。

I saw a cat crossing the road.

I saw a cat cross the road.

目的語の後に現在分詞がくる場合は継続中の動作や反復されている動作を表しているが，動詞の原形の場合は完了した動作を表し，事実そのものに重点が置かれる。

## 6．付帯状況を表す表現

付帯状況を表す形には with ＋名詞＋現在分詞や with ＋名詞＋過去分詞があるが，前者は名詞が「～して」という意味を，後者は名詞が「～されて」という受け身的な意味を持つ。

He was walking along the road with his dog following.

He sat there with his eyes closed.

上記の with ＋名詞で名詞の部分が主語と同一である場合 with は用いない。

He entered the room singing a song.

## 7．前置詞の後ろには不定詞節はこない

前置詞の後ろには名詞，代名詞，動名詞など名詞相当語句が生じ，文や不定詞節がくることはない。

I'm looking forward to the next party.

I'm looking forward to seeing you next Sunday.

## 8．go ＋～ing の注意点

go ＋～ing の形で go の後ろにくるものにはスポーツや娯楽に関するものがくることが多い。また，この表現に関して go の後ろは不定詞にはならないので注意。

go boating / go fishing / go camping / go riding / go shopping / go skating / go swimming / go walking / go dancing / go shooting

## 9．動名詞を用いた慣用表現

動名詞を用いた慣用表現で on ～ing は「～するやいなや」, in ～ing は「～する際」といった意味を持つ。

The thief ran away on seeing a policeman.（その泥棒は警官を見るやいなや逃げた）

Be careful in crossing the road.（その道路を横断する際には気をつけなさい）

## 10. 分詞構文の作り方

主節と従属節があり，主節と従属節の主語が同じ場合，接続詞と主語を省略し，動詞を分詞に直すと分詞構文が形成される。

When he had finished his homework, he went shopping.
　　　↓　　↓　　↓
　　　φ　　φ　Having finished his homework, he went shopping.

分詞構文が表す意味としては時（〜する時），原因・理由（〜なので），条件（〜ならば），譲歩（〜だけれども，たとえ〜しても），付帯状況（〜しながら，そして〜する）がある。また，主節と従属節の主語が異なる場合は接続詞だけを省略し，主語を残して動詞を分詞に変え独立分詞構文にする。

Night coming on, the typhoon swept the Kyushu area.

独立分詞構文の一種で熟語的な分詞構文として次のようなものがある。

generally speaking（一般的に言って）　strictly speaking（厳密に言って）　judging from（〜から判断すると）　talking of 〜（〜と言えば）　according to〜（〜によれば）　granted (granting) that 〜（仮に〜であるとしても）　provided (providing) 〜（もし〜であるなら）　supposing that（たとえ〜であっても）

## 練習問題

I．次の各文の（　）内の語を適当な形に変えなさい。
1．He spent the whole day (read) detective stories.
2．Would you mind (go) with me to the hospital?
3．He denied (have) written the letter.
4．I've never for one moment regretted (marry) her.
5．He felt a worm (crawl) over his arm.
6．He was found with his head (bury) among the rubbish.

7．(Judge) from the way he speaks, he must be a foreigner.
8．He saw his name (write) on the wall.
9．We gave up (try) to help him.
10．Why don't we go (skate) on Lake Suwa?

Ⅱ．次の各文の誤りを訂正しなさい。
1．I remember to see the watch, but I have no idea where to look for it.
2．We are all looking forward to hear the news of his marriage.
3．He promised trying hard, but he failed.
4．Badly injuring in the leg, he could not walk any more.
5．The boy raised his left hand is our child.

Ⅲ．日本語に合うように（　　）内に適切な英語を入れなさい。
1．彼は忘れずにその文書を委員会に提出したが，それにはいくつか不備があった。
　　He (　　) to submit the document to the committee, but there were a few (　　) in it.
2．私は若い頃怠けていたことを後悔したが手遅れだった。
　　I repented too (　　) of having been (　　) when I was young.
3．彼らの会話はドイツ語だったので私たちは彼らの言うことが分からなかった。
　　Their conversation being (　　) German, we could not understand (　　) they were talking about.
4．その時は天気がよかったので窓を開けたままにしておきました。
　　The weather being (　　), I kept the door (　　).
5．私はこの手紙を出すのを忘れていたため，妻に叱られてしまった。
　　As I forgot (　　) this letter, my wife scolded me.

**Ⅳ．次の日本語を英語にしなさい。**

1．車を運転する時は運転免許証を携帯していなければなりません。
2．一般的に言って音韻論（phonology）は言語学において基本的な分野である。
3．ドアのところに着くとすぐ彼は静かにドアを開けた。
4．口に食べ物を一杯にしてものを言ってはいけません。
5．彼は寸時も目を離さず彼女が踊っている姿を見ていた。

# Chapter 14　比　較

## 1．1音節の語の比較級，最上級

1音節の語は原級に -er を付けて比較級にし，-est を付けて最上級にする。

young-younger-youngest / fast-faster-fastest / deep-deeper-deepest / long-longer-longest

## 2．2音節以上の語の比較級，最上級

2音節以上の語は比較級に more，最上級に most を付けることが多いが，-er, -le, -y, -ow, -some で終わる語には -er, -est を付ける。

tender-tenderer-tenderest / simple-simpler-simplest / shallow-shallower-shallowest / handsome-handsomer-handsomest

また early を除き -ly で終わる副詞にはすべて more や most を付ける。

more slowly　most slowly / more kindly　most kindly / more quickly　most quickly

## 3．3音節以上の語の比較級，最上級

3音節以上の語はすべて more や most を前に置く。

more intelligent　most intelligent / more easily　most easily

## 4．最上級 last の用法

last が「最近の」，「最新の」という意味を表すことがある。

This is the last letter I received from my mother.

## 5. 原級, 比較級を修飾するもの

原級を修飾するものは very で, 比較級を修飾するものは much, even, far, by far, still, a little である。

　○ He is much older than I.

　× He is very older than I.

## 6. than の後ろの省略構文

同等比較の as と同じように than の後にも通常省略構文が続く。

　He is smarter than I (am).

　He speaks French better than I (speak French).

また He likes her more than you. のような文は次のように省略される部分が異なる場合がある。

　He likes her more than you (like her).

　He likes her more than (he likes) you.

前者の場合は次のように代動詞を用いて曖昧さを避ける。

　He likes her more than you do.

## 7. ラテン語起源の比較級

ラテン語起源の比較級 (superior, inferior, senior, junior, prior など) の後ろには than ではなく to がくる。

　He is five years senior to me.

　She is five years junior to me.

## 8. 比較の対象となるものの数とその表現

2人または2つの物を比較する場合, the ＋比較級＋ of the two のように比較級を使い, 3人または3つ以上の物を比較する場合は, the ＋最上級＋ of the three のように最上級を使う。

　This package is the heavier of the two.

This package is the heaviest of the three.

## 9．「～より少ない」という表現の注意点

「～より少ない」という表現で数に関する場合は fewer を，量に関する場合は less を使う。

John has few books in English.

John has less information than Bill.

## 10. 同一の人または物の性質を比較する場合

同一の人または物の性質を比較する場合，原級 + er 形は使わず more を使う。

He is more kind than generous.

He is more dead than alive.


### 練習問題

Ⅰ．次の（　）内の語を適当な形に直しなさい。
1．He looks (happy) when he is speaking with his wife.
2．Lucy is the (pretty) of the two girls.
3．My father is (little) old than you think he is.
4．Today's examination is the (difficult) of all that we have ever taken.
5．In spring the days grow (long) and it gets (warm).

Ⅱ．次の各文の誤りを訂正しなさい。
1．Baseball is preferable than football in our school.
2．He is three years senior than I.
3．He is more badly off than he was five years ago.

4．The salesman is wiser than kind.
5．This picture is the best of the two he has painted.

Ⅲ．日本語に合うように（　　）内に適切な英語を入れなさい。
1．この川の幅はあの川の約半分です。
　This river is about (　　) as broad (　　) that river.
2．彼は私より10歳年下ですが，処世術をよく心得ています。
　Though he is ten years (　　) to me, he knows well how to get (　　) in life.
3．彼は学業的業績においては私より優れているが，経験では私より劣っている。
　He is (　　) to me in academic achievement, but is (　　) to me in experience.
4．あなたも彼と同じくらい悪いのです。
　You are as (　　) to blame as he is.
5．彼は私が思ったよりいい論文を提出しました。
　He submitted a better paper than I (　　).

Ⅳ．次の日本語を英語にしなさい。
1．彼は数年前より暮らし向きがよくなっています。
2．あなたは私ぐらいの年になれば，人生経験を積むことが必要であることが分かるでしょう。
3．私は彼女に感謝しているのと同じくらい彼にも感謝している。
4．その二つの本のうちどちらが論文を書く際に役立ちますか。
5．これは私がこれまでに見た中で1番印象的な景色です。

# Chapter 15　その他注意すべき構文

1．否定語が文頭にある時の語順

　否定語の意味を強めるためにそれを文頭に移動させると，疑問文で見られる主語・助動詞倒置が生じる。

　　Never did I expect to see you in this place.

　　If you don't go, neither shall I go.

2．x (a + b) という関係

　1つの語句が2つ以上の語句のいずれにも等しくかかり x (a + b) といった形が形成される場合がある。

　　Democracy is the government of the people, by the people, and for the people.

　■次のような例では (a + b) x といった形になっている。

　　We can derive at least some, maybe all, of the intricate properties of the material.

3．状態を表す二次的な述語

　ある行為・動作に伴うまたはその結果生じる状態を be 動詞類を用いずに後ろに置いて表す場合がある。

　　He entered the room angry.

　　He fell down unconscious.

　　He died young.

## 4．結果を表す二次的な述語

ある行為・動作が目的語に作用し，それに伴って目的語がある状態になる場合，be動詞類を用いずに目的語の後ろにその状態を表す語を置く場合がある。

　　He hammered the metal flat.
　　He stroke the dog dead.

## 5．文字通り英語にできない動詞

自動詞の中には日本語を文字通り英語にしても意味をなさない場合がある。

　　Your nose is running.（鼻水が流れる）　　His plan did not succeed.（うまく行かなかった）　　This machine doesn't work.（動かない）　　Your voice carries well.（声が通る）　　This cake sells well.（よく売れる）　　Things went according to plan.（運んだ）

## 6．理由を表す従属節

Becauseで始まる従属節が後ろにくる場合，前の節をピリオドで区切ってbecause節を独立させることはできない。また，接続詞のforは前の文を受けて理由を表すが，文頭にくることはない。

　○ She was drowned because she fell off the pier.
　× She was drowned. Because she fell off the pier.
　○ I must be going, for I have my own business to attend to.
　× For I have my own business to attend to, I must be going.

## 7．名詞を修飾する形容詞の語順

名詞を修飾する形容詞が幾つか並ぶときはその順序は原則として冠詞・代名詞類，数量，大小・長短，性質，色彩，年齢・新旧，所属・材料のようになる。

the three red rose / these five young American students / a long black new woolen scarf

## 8．間接疑問文の語順

普通の疑問文では What are you doing? のように主語・助動詞倒置が生じるが，間接疑問文においては主語・助動詞倒置は生じない。

○ I wonder where my dog is.

× I wonder where is my dog.

## 9．-thing, -body, -one で終わる語と修飾語

-thing, -body, -one で終わる語を修飾する場合それらは後置される。

○ something cold to drink / somebody rich

× cold something to drink / rich somebody

## 10.「私と彼」は英語では he and I

日本語で「私と彼」また「彼と私」と言えるが，英語では自分の方は後ろに置かれ he and I となる。また，親子関係を表す場合親の方を先に置くのが普通である。

○ she and I / father and son / mother and daughter

× I and she / son and father / daughter and mother

## 練習問題

Ⅰ．次の（　）内から正しい語を選びなさい。

1．This computer doesn't (work, move).
2．Little (I, did I) dream of becoming a politician.
3．The child was born (dead, be dead).
4．A door banged (open, opened).

5．Storms often (come, occur) in winter.

Ⅱ．次の各文の誤りを訂正しなさい。
1．I wonder when will the letter reach me.
2．You didn't attend the meeting and I neither did.
3．I and my brother would often go fishing.
4．She is proud of her golden soft long hair.
5．He had particular nothing to do yesterday.

Ⅲ．日本語に合うように（　　）内に適切な英語を入れなさい。
1．珍しい絵の中には非常に高い値で売れるものがある。
　　Some rare pictures (　　) at a very high price.
2．動物園から昨日逃げ出した虎は生け捕りになった。
　　The tiger which ran (　　) from the zoo yesterday was caught (　　).
3．昨日の寒い天気で木の葉が紅葉してしまった。
　　Yesterday's cold weather turned the leaves (　　).
4．彼は決して間食をしない。
　　Never does he eat between (　　).
5．彼はたくさんコンピュータを持っているが，コンピュータおたくではないと言った。
　　He said that he had a lot of computer, but (　　) he was not a computer nerd.

Ⅳ．次の日本語を英語にしなさい。
1．彼はその知的な年をとった英国の芸術家を牧師と間違えた。
2．私たちが子供の頃学んだ学校はどうなっているかしら。
3．私と彼は大学時代からの友達ですが，彼を知っている人はだれでも気むずかしい男だと言います。

4．明日は雨が降るでしょう。というのはあの山が雲に覆われているから。
5．今日の新聞には何か面白いものがありますか。

# 語　彙

**1．日用品に関する語彙**

1．爪切り（　）　2．練り歯磨き（　）　3．ワイシャツ（　）
4．実印（　）　5．判子（　）　6．洗剤（　）　7．漂白剤（　）
8．ゴミ箱（　）　9．電気掃除機（　）　10．目薬（　）

①garbage can　②nail clipper　③seal　④legal seal　⑤eyewash
⑥bleach　⑦vacuum cleaner　⑧dress shirt　⑨toothpaste　⑩detergent

**2．文房具に関する語彙**

1．万年筆（　）　2．ボールペン（　）　3．マジックペン（　）
4．シャープペンシル（　）　5．消しゴム（　）　6．修正液（　）
7．定規（　）　8．ホチキス（　）　9．糊（　）　10．セロテープ（　）

①paste　②mechanical pencil　③eraser　④whitewash　⑤stapler
⑥cellophane tape　⑦ruler　⑧felt marker　⑨fountain pen
⑩ballpoint pen

**3．食品に関する語彙**

1．加工食品（　）　2．保存食品（　）　3．ドライフード（　）
4．レトルト食品（　）　5．人工着色料（　）　6．食品保存添加物（　）
7．賞味期限（　）　8．食べ残し（　）　9．外食（　）
10．ドリンク剤（　）

①use-by date　②leftover　③processed foods　④dehydrated foods
⑤artificial coloring agent　⑥dining out　⑦preserved foods
⑧retort pouch foods　⑨food preservative　⑩quick-fix drink

## 4．鉄道に関する語彙
1．地下鉄（ ）　2．急行列車（ ）　3．電車賃（ ）
4．片道切符（ ）　5．往復切符（ ）　6．乗り換え切符（ ）
7．乗車口（ ）　8．発車ホーム（ ）　9．途中下車する（ ）
10．乗り換える（ ）

①way-in　②one-way ticket　③stop over　④subway (tube, underground)
⑤express　⑥departure platform　⑦round-trip ticket
⑧transfer-ticket　⑨change trains (transfer)　⑩train fare

## 5．犯罪に関する語彙(1)
1．犯罪者（ ）　2．被害者（ ）　3．容疑者（ ）　4．目撃者（ ）
5．殺人事件（ ）　6．傷害（ ）　7．強盗（ ）　8．窃盗（ ）
9．恐喝（ ）　10．誘拐（ ）

①injury　②abduction　③murder case　④suspect　⑤criminal
⑥eyewitness　⑦theft　⑧blackmail　⑨burglary (robbery)　⑩victim

## 6．犯罪に関する語彙(2)
1．ひったくり（ ）　2．詐欺（ ）　3．万引き（ ）　4．暴行（ ）
5．横領（ ）　6．密輸入（ ）　7．密航者（ ）　8．偽証（ ）
9．放火（ ）　10．青少年犯罪（ ）

①stowaway　②bag-snatching　③assault　④embezzlement　⑤perjury
⑥swindle (fraud)　⑦arson　⑧juvenile delinquency　⑨shoplifting
⑩smuggling

## 7．犯罪に関する語彙(3)
1．痴漢（ ）　2．死刑（ ）　3．無期懲役（ ）　4．重罪（ ）
5．殺人罪（ ）　6．執行猶予（ ）　7．前科者（ ）　8．人質（ ）
9．身代金（ ）　10．過失致死罪（ ）

① ex-convict  ② molester  ③ probation  ④ life imprisonment
⑤ capital punishment  ⑥ accidental homicide  ⑦ felony  ⑧ homicide
⑨ ransom  ⑩ hostage

## 8．科学技術に関する語彙
1．集積回路（　）　2．共鳴（　）　3．陽極（　）　4．重力（　）
5．陰極（　）　6．交流（　）　7．直流（　）　8．絶縁体（　）
9．電流（　）　10．放電（　）

① anode  ② direct current  ③ resonation  ④ gravity
⑤ electric discharge  ⑥ insulator  ⑦ electric current  ⑧ negative pole
⑨ integrated circuit  ⑩ alternating current

## 9．化学に関する語彙(1)
1．液体（　）　2．液化（　）　3．化合物（　）　4．還元（　）
5．気化（　）　6．合成（　）　7．混合物（　）　8．酸化（　）
9．酸性（　）　10．昇華（　）

① reduction  ② oxidation  ③ sublimation  ④ mixture  ⑤ vaporization
⑥ liquefaction  ⑦ compound  ⑧ liquid  ⑨ acidity  ⑩ synthesis

## 10．化学に関する語彙(2)
1．蒸発（　）　2．水溶液（　）　3．中和（　）　4．沈殿（　）
5．濃度（　）　6．飽和（　）　7．融解（　）　8．溶液（　）
9．溶解（　）　10．溶剤（　）

① solution  ② precipitation  ③ saturation  ④ concentration
⑤ evaporation  ⑥ dissolution  ⑦ solvent  ⑧ aqueous solution
⑨ neutralization  ⑩ fusion

## 11. 電話に関する語彙

1. 国番号（ ）　2. 交換手（ ）　3. 公衆電話（ ）
4. 国際電話（ ）　5. 留守番電話（ ）　6. フリーダイアル（ ）
7. 市外局番（ ）　8. 市内電話（ ）　9. 長距離電話（ ）
10. 内線（ ）

①answering machine　②area code　③country code　④extension
⑤international call　⑥local call　⑦long distance call　⑧operator
⑨pay phone　⑩toll-free number

## 12. 気候に関する語彙(1)

1. 湿度（ ）　2. 気温（ ）　3. 梅雨（ ）　4. 台風（ ）
5. 変わりやすい（ ）　6. 曇り（ ）　7. 降水量（ ）
8. 積雪量（ ）　9. 雷（ ）　10. 温度計（ ）

①thunder　②changeable　③typhoon　④precipitation　⑤temperature
⑥thermometer　⑦cloudy　⑧rainy season　⑨humidity　⑩snowfall

## 13. 気候に関する語彙(2)

1. 温帯（ ）　2. 熱帯（ ）　3. 蒸し暑い（ ）　4. 竜巻（ ）
5. ハリケーン（ ）　6. 干ばつ（ ）　7. みぞれ（ ）
8. 平均気温（ ）　9. 雷雨（ ）　10. なだれ（ ）

①thunderstorm　②hurricane　③drought　④avalanche　⑤sleet
⑥muggy　⑦the temperate zone　⑧tornado　⑨the tropics
⑩average temperature

## 14. 気候に関する語彙(3)

1. 摂氏（ ）　2. 華氏（ ）　3. 寒波（ ）　4. 熱波（ ）
5. 霧雨（ ）　6. 小春日和（ ）　7. かすみ（ ）　8. 低気圧（ ）
9. 高気圧（ ）　10. 暴風雨（ ）

①mist ②Indian summer ③heat wave ④drizzle ⑤cold wave
⑥Celsius ⑦Fahrenheit ⑧tempest ⑨depression ⑩high pressure

### 15. 郵便に関する語彙(1)
1．印刷物（ ）　2．消印（ ）　3．小包（ ）　4．差出人（ ）
5．受取人（ ）　6．船便（ ）　7．郵便受け（ ）　8．同封する（ ）
9．着払いで（ ）　10．転送住所（ ）

①sender ②addressee ③surface mail ④forwarding address
⑤enclose ⑥postmark ⑦mailbox ⑧parcel
⑨C.O.D. (cash on delivery) ⑩printed matter

### 16. 郵便に関する語彙(2)
1．航空便（ ）　2．国内郵便（ ）　3．私書箱（ ）
4．取扱注意（ ）　5．返信料（ ）　6．郵便為替（ ）
7．速達（ ）　8．切手（ ）　9．壊れ物（ ）
10．～様方；～気付け（ ）

①stamp ②handle with care ③money order ④P.O. Box
⑤return postage ⑥domestic mail ⑦care of; c/o ⑧special delivery
⑨airmail ⑩fragile

### 17. 郵便に関する語彙(3)
1．配達（ ）　2．保険（ ）　3．郵便番号（ ）　4．郵便料金（ ）
5．書留（ ）　6．往復はがき（ ）　7．局留め郵便（ ）
8．料金別納郵便（ ）　9．送金（ ）　10．受取人指定郵便（ ）

①general delivery ②registered mail ③reply-paid postcard
④restricted delivery ⑤zip code ⑥insurance ⑦remittance
⑧delivery ⑨postage ⑩metered mail

## 18. 学校に関する語彙(1)

1．学年（　）　2．掲示板（　）　3．実験室（　）　4．学用品（　）
5．幼稚園（　）　6．小学校（　）　7．遅刻（　）　8．転校する（　）
9．義務教育（　）　10．欠席（　）

①absence　②kindergarten　③compulsory education
④elementary school　⑤transfer　⑥bulletin board　⑦grade　⑧tardy
⑨laboratory　⑩school supplies

## 19. 学校に関する語彙(2)

1．男女共学（　）　2．制服（　）　3．学位（　）　4．教育費（　）
5．講堂（　）　6．出席（　）　7．専門学校（　）　8．予備校（　）
9．体育館（　）　10．いじめ（　）

①attendance　②degree　③bullying　④gymnasium　⑤school uniform
⑥vocational school　⑦educational expenses　⑧auditorium
⑨preparatory school　⑩coeducation

## 20. 学校に関する語彙(3)

1．単位（　）　2．入学許可（　）　3．学業成績証明書（　）
4．卒業式（　）　5．偏差値（　）　6．奨学金（　）　7．出席簿（　）
8．内申書（　）　9．学期（　）　10．授業料（　）

①semester (term)　②tuition　③commencement　④deviation value
⑤school report　⑥roll book　⑦fellowship　⑧admission　⑨credit
⑩transcript

## 21. 学問に関する語彙(1)

1．経済学（　）　2．哲学（　）　3．文学（　）　4．心理学（　）
5．政治学（　）　6．天文学（　）　7．経営学（　）　8．社会学（　）
9．人類学（　）　10．生物学（　）

① astronomy　② biology　③ philosophy　④ sociology　⑤ psychology
⑥ anthropology　⑦ literature　⑧ political science　⑨ economics
⑩ business administration

### 22. 学問に関する語彙(2)
1．工学（　）　2．美学（　）　3．代数学（　）　4．考古学（　）
5．倫理学（　）　6．動物学（　）　7．地質学（　）　8．言語学（　）
9．数学（　）　10．物理学（　）

① mathematics　② engineering　③ algebra　④ ethics　⑤ linguistics
⑥ aesthetics　⑦ physics　⑧ archeology　⑨ zoology　⑩ geology

### 23. 病名に関する語彙(1)
1．貧血（　）　2．拒食症（　）　3．過食症（　）　4．盲腸炎（　）
5．関節炎（　）　6．神経痛（　）　7．ぜんそく（　）　8．水虫（　）
9．脳出血（　）　10．虫歯（　）

① brain hemorrhage　② asthma　③ athlete's foot　④ appendicitis
⑤ neuralgia　⑥ anemia　⑦ anorexia　⑧ bulimia　⑨ cavity　⑩ arthritis

### 24. 病名に関する語彙(2)
1．昏睡（　）　2．けいれん（　）　3．膀胱炎（　）　4．うつ病（　）
5．下痢（　）　6．骨折（　）　7．胃潰瘍（　）　8．二日酔い（　）
9．花粉症（　）　10．胸焼け（　）

① convulsion　② fracture　③ heartburn　④ gastric ulcer　⑤ hangover
⑥ depression　⑦ diarrhea　⑧ hay fever　⑨ cystitis　⑩ coma

### 25. 病名に関する語彙(3)
1．高血圧（　）　2．不眠症（　）　3．白血病（　）　4．はしか（　）
5．偏頭痛（　）　6．生理（　）　7．肺炎（　）　8．日射病（　）

9．めまい（　）　10．嘔吐（　）

①insomnia　②vertigo (dizziness)　③period　④sunstroke　⑤vomiting
⑥measles　⑦leukemia　⑧migraine　⑨hypertension　⑩pneumonia

## 26．医者に関する語彙
1．皮膚科医（　）　2．眼科医（　）　3．整形外科医（　）
4．婦人科医（　）　5．小児科医（　）　6．内科医（　）
7．外科医（　）　8．泌尿器科医（　）　9．耳鼻咽喉科医（　）
10．精神科医（　）

①pediatrician　②dermatologist　③gynecologist　④psychiatrist
⑤otorhinolaryngologist　⑥surgeon　⑦urologist　⑧ophthalmologist
⑨physician　⑩orthopedist

## 27．人体に関する語彙
1．脳（　）　2．食道（　）　3．胆嚢（　）　4．腎臓（　）
5．肝臓（　）　6．膵臓（　）　7．喉頭（　）　8．関節（　）
9．脊髄（　）　10．脾臓（　）

①spinal cord　②brain　③spleen　④larynx　⑤joint　⑥pancreas
⑦liver　⑧gullet　⑨gall bladder　⑩kidney

## 28．職業に関する語彙(1)
1．会社員（　）　2．建築家（　）　3．受付係（　）　4．パン屋（　）
5．美容師（　）　6．仕立屋（　）　7．修理工（　）　8．花屋（　）
9．消防士（　）　10．肉屋（　）

①fire fighter　②florist　③butcher　④tailor　⑤mechanic　⑥baker
⑦hairdresser　⑧office worker　⑨architect　⑩receptionist

## 29. 職業に関する語彙(2)

1. 不動産屋（ ）　2. 理容師（ ）　3. 会計士（ ）　4. 刑事（ ）
5. 大工（ ）　6. 秘書（ ）　7. 弁護士（ ）　8. 薬剤師（ ）
9. 旅行業者（ ）　10. 眼鏡屋（ ）

① carpenter　② optician　③ lawyer　④ accountant　⑤ secretary
⑥ pharmacist　⑦ detective　⑧ travel agent　⑨ real estate agent
⑩ barber

## 30. 海外旅行に関する語彙(1)

1. 出発（ ）　2. 手荷物（ ）　3. 搭乗手続き（ ）
4. 機内の荷物入れ（ ）　5. 税関申告書（ ）　6. 国籍（ ）
7. 目的地（ ）　8. 出国カード（ ）　9. 入国カード（ ）
10. 現地時間（ ）

① nationality　② destination　③ embarkation card
④ disembarkation card　⑤ overhead compartment　⑥ departure
⑦ customs declaration card　⑧ local time　⑨ check in　⑩ baggage

## 31. 海外旅行に関する語彙(2)

1. 出入国カード（ ）　2. 税関検査（ ）　3. 手荷物受取所（ ）
4. 手荷物引換券（ ）　5. 搭乗券（ ）　6. 関税（ ）
7. 超過手荷物（ ）　8. 出入国管理事務所（ ）　9. 検疫（ ）
10. 手荷物検査（ ）

① quarantine　② immigration card　③ security screening
④ customs duties　⑤ immigration　⑥ baggage claim tags
⑦ boarding pass　⑧ customs inspection　⑨ baggage claim area
⑩ excess baggage

## 32. 政治に関する語彙(1)

1．首相（　）　2．内閣（　）　3．行政（　）　4．政府（　）
5．連立内閣（　）　6．行政改革（　）　7．大臣（　）　8．閣僚（　）
9．任命（　）　10．自治（　）

①minister　②administration　③Cabinet minister
④administrative reform　⑤prime minister　⑥coalition Cabinet
⑦autonomy　⑧appointment　⑨government　⑩Cabinet

## 33. 政治に関する語彙(2)

1．二院制（　）　2．選挙（　）　3．選挙権（　）　4．補欠選挙（　）
5．予算委員会（　）　6．選挙民（　）　7．選挙区（　）
8．選挙運動（　）　9．立候補（　）　10．立候補者（　）

①election　②electorate　③candidate　④constituency
⑤bicameral system　⑥budget committee　⑦candidacy　⑧by-election
⑨suffrage　⑩election campaign

## 34. 政治に関する語彙(3)

1．国会（　）　2．現職者（　）　3．解散（　）　4．衆議院（　）
5．参議院（　）　6．与党（　）　7．野党（　）　8．政党（　）
9．決定票（　）　10．不信任投票（　）

①ruling party　②the Diet　③dissolution　④incumbent
⑤the House of Representative　⑥the House of Councilors
⑦vote of nonconfidence　⑧casting vote　⑨opposition party
⑩political party

## 35. 政治に関する語彙(4)

1．立法（　）　2．立法権（　）　3．本会議（　）　4．議会制（　）
5．不在投票（　）　6．有権者（　）　7．選挙遊説（　）

8．開票結果（　）　9．投票所（　）　10．国民投票（　）

①eligible voter　②polling station　③absentee vote　④campaign trial
⑤referendum　⑥election returns　⑦legislation　⑧plenary session
⑨parliamentary system　⑩legislative power

## 36. 経済に関する語彙(1)
1．経済成長（　）　2．景気（　）　3．景気回復（　）　4．国債（　）
5．市場経済（　）　6．経済制裁（　）　7．開放経済（　）
8．黒字（　）　9．赤字（　）　10．国民所得（　）

①open economy　②surplus　③national income　④business　⑤deficit
⑥economic growth　⑦economic sanctions　⑧business recovery
⑨market economy　⑩government bond

## 37. 経済に関する語彙(2)
1．金融政策（　）　2．金融緩和（　）　3．円高（　）　4．円安（　）
5．株式市場（　）　6．金融市場（　）　7．公共投資（　）
8．公共支出（　）　9．公定歩合（　）　10．投資（　）

①appreciation of yen　②depreciation of yen　③financial policy
④public investment　⑤official discount rate　⑥stock market
⑦public expenditure　⑧monetary ease　⑨investment　⑩money market

## 38. 経済に関する語彙(3)
1．証券取引所（　）　2．投機（　）　3．国際収支（　）
4．貿易収支（　）　5．元金（　）　6．純益（　）　7．歳入（　）
8．歳出（　）　9．現金払い（　）　10．配当（　）

①pay-as-you-go system　②principal　③net income　④dividend
⑤speculation　⑥stock exchange　⑦revenue　⑧balance of payments
⑨expenditure　⑩trade balance

### 39. 宗教に関する語彙(1)
1．信仰（　）　2．仏教（　）　3．禅宗（　）　4．神道（　）
5．儒教（　）　6．道教（　）　7．ヒンズー教（　）8．イスラム教（　）
9．キリスト教（　）　10．キリスト教徒（　）

①Islam (Islamism)　②faith　③Hinduism　④Christian　⑤Christianity
⑥Confucianism　⑦Shinto (Shintoism)　⑧Taoism　⑨Buddhism
⑩Zen Buddhism

### 40. 宗教に関する語彙(2)
1．教義（　）　2．崇拝（　）　3．無神論者（　）　4．教祖（　）
5．安息日（　）　6．経典（　）　7．新興宗教（　）　8．洗礼（　）
9．聖職者（　）　10．神学者（　）

①clergy　②theologian　③atheist　④guru　⑤doctrine　⑥baptism
⑦scripture (sutra)　⑧Sabbath　⑨worship　⑩cult

### 41. ビジネスに関する語彙(1)
1．本社（　）　2．支店（　）　3．年金（　）　4．定年退職（　）
5．有給休暇（　）　6．就職口（　）　7．人件費（　）　8．夜勤（　）
9．ストライキ（　）　10．会長（　）

①job opening　②personnel cost　③Chief Executive Officer (CEO)
④the night shift　⑤paid vacation　⑥pension　⑦head office　⑧walkout
⑨branch office　⑩mandatory retirement

### 42. ビジネスに関する語彙(2)
1．通勤手当（　）　2．残業手当（　）　3．失業手当（　）
4．履歴書（　）　5．求人広告（　）　6．セット料金（　）
7．処分セール（　）　8．儲かる商品（　）　9．目玉商品（　）
10．売上高（　）

①clearance sale　②loss leader　③unemployment allowance　④resume
⑤classified ad　⑥proceeds　⑦cash cow　⑧commuting allowance
⑨overtime allowance　⑩unit price

## 43. ビジネスに関する語彙(3)

1．労働組合（　）　2．業務日誌（　）　3．ちらし（　）　4．明細（　）
5．債権者（　）　6．督促状（　）　7．特許権（　）　8．合併（　）
9．高額商品（　）　10．薄利多売（　）

①leaflet　②low-margin high-turnover　③amalgamation　④labor union
⑤breakdown　⑥creditor　⑦high-ticket item　⑧log　⑨reminder
⑩royalty

## 44. 図形に関する語彙(1)

1．円（　）　2．楕円（　）　3．扇形（　）　4．正方形（　）
5．長方形（　）　6．ひし形（　）　7．五角形（　）　8．六角形（　）
9．七角形（　）　10．八角形（　）

①square　②pentagon　③oval　④circle　⑤rectangle　⑥hexagon
⑦diamond　⑧octagon　⑨heptagon　⑩sector

## 45. 図形に関する語彙(2)

1．台形（　）　2．立方体（　）　3．球（　）　4．円柱（　）
5．円錐（　）　6．四面体（　）　7．角錐（　）　8．四角錐（　）
9．展開図（　）　10．二等辺三角形（　）

①pyramid　②cylinder　③trapezoid　④cone　⑤development　⑥cube
⑦sphere　⑧prism　⑨tetrahedron　⑩isosceles triangle

## 46. 数学に関する語彙(1)

1．比例（　）　2．正比例（　）　3．反比例（　）　4．長さ（　）

5．重さ（ ）　6．面積（ ）　7．体積（ ）　8．底辺（ ）
9．頂点（ ）　10．円周（ ）

①length　②volume　③proportion　④vertex　⑤base
⑥direct proportion　⑦inverse proportion　⑧weight　⑨circumference
⑩area

### 47. 数学に関する語彙(2)
1．半径（ ）　2．直径（ ）　3．接線（ ）　4．接点（ ）
5．角度（ ）　6．中心角（ ）　7．内角（ ）　8．外角（ ）
9．放物線（ ）　10．座標（ ）

①tangential line　②center angle　③coordinates　④interior angle
⑤angle　⑥parabola　⑦exterior angle　⑧radius　⑨diameter
⑩point of contact

### 48. 数学に関する語彙(3)
1．関数（ ）　2．因数（ ）　3．整数（ ）　4．実数（ ）
5．偶数（ ）　6．奇数（ ）　7．四捨五入する（ ）
8．切り上げる（ ）　9．横（幅）（ ）　10．高さ（ ）

①real number　②factor　③function　④odd number　⑤integer
⑥height　⑦even number　⑧round up　⑨width　⑩round off

### 49. 数学に関する語彙(4)
1．奥行き（ ）　2．足し算（ ）　3．引き算（ ）　4．かけ算（ ）
5．わり算（ ）　6．等式（ ）　7．最大公約数（ ）
8．最小公倍数（ ）　9．平行線（ ）　10．対角線（ ）

①greatest common divisor　②multiplication　③addition
④least common multiple　⑤subtraction　⑥depth　⑦diagonal line
⑧parallel line　⑨equation　⑩division

## 50. グラフに関する語彙

1．図形（　）　2．ベン図（　）　3．円グラフ（　）
4．度数分布図（　）　5．線グラフ（　）　6．放物線グラフ（　）
7．棒グラフ（　）　8．絵グラフ（　）　9．樹形図（　）
10．流れ図（　）

① pictograph　② histogram　③ diagram　④ line graph　⑤ bar graph
⑥ Venn diagram　⑦ parabolic graph　⑧ flow chart　⑨ pie chart
⑩ tree diagram

## 練習問題の解答

### Chapter 1　句読法

Ⅰ.
1. Don't you think you have had enough steak?
2. Would you like some coffee?
3. If you hurry up, you will be in time for the train.
4. My youngest uncle, who lives in New York, is a doctor.
5. I lived in Tampa, Florida.
6. Gentlemen, please!
7. He hoped that she would come with his mother and that they would make an apple pie for him.
8. This book, if you read it well, will greatly benefit you.
9. On May 7, 1945, Germany proclaimed the unconditional surrender to the Allies.
10. In 1995, he married Jane, a woman seven or eight years older than himself.
11. He tried to solve the problem, for he could not go ahead without a solution.
12. He sought a solution ; however, all his efforts failed.
13. Water consists of two elements : oxygen and hydrogen.
14. He cried, "Help me out."
15. Before dinner, on the terrace, they spent an hour.
16. Little can be said for the book ; the author doesn't know rhetoric.
17. He wrote more than fifty plays in verse (one of the most frequently used forms in the 17th century).
18. The village where he lives is famous for its production of orange.
19. *Atami*, where I went for change of air a few years ago, is within reach of Tokyo.
20. He bought a new house, which he has lately moved into.

Ⅱ.
1. "Something is wrong with my stomach these days." "That's too bad."
2. Shakespeare was the most popular dramatist in the Elizabethan age, and few dramatists in the world could equal him in popularity.
3. The United Kingdom is made up of four different regions : England, Scotland, Wales, and Northern Ireland.
4. Turn to the right at the next corner, and you will find the station in the left side.
5. Taro left Tokyo and started for New York March 5, 1998.

Ⅲ.
1. This food has been developed for people who cannot reduce the amount of a meal they have.
2. I often go to Oita Prefecture, where a hot-spring resort is famous.
3. Hemingway, a noted American novelist, wrote not only long stories (full-length novels) but also short stories.
4. He said, "You would have done the same thing, if you had been in my place."
5. Did you remember to take your medicine before dinner? If not, you had better take it now.

**Chapter 2　名詞(1)**
Ⅰ.
1. letters
2. glasses
3. manners
4. two pieces of furniture
5. customers

Ⅱ.
1. My father gave me good advice.
2. Yesterday I met one of my old friends.
3. Please give me three pieces of chalk.
4. We got through customs before we were admitted into the country.
5. The clergy are opposing the bill.

Ⅲ.
1. The tennis player underestimated the opponent and lost.
2. He was transferred to parts, so he left his family behind in Tokyo.
3. The cattle were dying because they had no grass to eat.
4. I cannot go out today because I have to do my math homework for tomorrow.
5. How many pieces of baggage can I take on the airplane with me?

Ⅳ.
1. It is bad manners to make noises at table.
2. He put three spoonfuls of sugar into his coffee.
3. The student wearing glasses is quite tall for his age.
4. The flood the other day caused a lot of damage to the town.
5. He is the greatest man of letters in Japan.

**Chapter 3　名詞(2)**

Ⅰ.
1. the other
2. take
3. another
4. time
5. tongue

Ⅱ.
1. He climbed the mountain with ease.
2. A good idea came to my mind last night.
3. He shook his head in disapproval in discussing the pay raise at the meeting.
4. Please keep this wine in this refrigerator for another ten minutes.
5. There were a large audience in the concert hall.

Ⅲ.
1. Three of the ten competitors won prizes ; the others got nothing.
2. Some people are fond of going out ; others prefer staying indoors to watch TV.
3. My opinion differs from that of most people.
4. He tried vainly to find his watch with keeping an eye open.
5. He has gone to the United States on business.

Ⅳ.
1. When he gave me a present yesterday, I could not believe my eyes.
2. He has a loose tongue, so you had better not say to him whatever you think.
3. "Why don't we go hiking to the country next Sunday?"
   "Next Sunday will not suit me well."
4. She saved five million yen for a rainy day when she worked in an office.
5. He was reading a book lying on his back.

**Chapter 4　冠詞(1)**

Ⅰ.
1. a
2. a
3. the
4. the, a
5. a, The, the

Ⅱ.
1. What kind of book do you have?

2. We ate chicken at the restaurant.
3. The car can run 100 miles an hour.
4. We are all of an age.
5. An eagle is a bird of prey.

Ⅲ.
1. He writes to his parents at home once a week.
2. Bill is American and the rest of us are German.
3. He is not the sort of man to do such a thing.
4. It is true that the sun rises in the east and sets in the west.
5. At the beginning of autumn when it gets colder day by day and the days get shorter, we usually have settled weather.

Ⅳ.
1. The earth on which we live is spherical in shape and its surface consists of sea and land.
2. If you see him once, you will see he is a man of sincerity.
3. A whale is a mammal.
4. He said that he was not sure whether he had left his umbrella in the train or in the bus.
5. Whether you have a lot of money or a little money does not matter. The problem is how you use the money you have now.

## Chapter 5　冠詞(2)
Ⅰ.
1. the, the
2. the
3. the, the
4. the
5. the

Ⅱ.
1. Are you going to Tokyo by car?
2. He works hard night and day.
3. Have you eaten dinner yet?
4. If you commit a crime, you will be sent to prison.
5. Suddenly I came face to face with Professor Jones.

Ⅲ.
1. The brothers have the same merits and the same faults.
2. How much does it cost to go from Tokyo to London by plane?
3. Humans can produce novel sentences whenever they want to.

4. This is the company where he once worked as an interpreter.
5. He makes it a rule to sleep in the daytime and wake up at night to set about writing.

Ⅳ.
1. Someone approached me and patted me on the shoulder.
2. They came roaring arm in arm.
3. Though the rumor was that some of them were bribed, he was elected mayor of New York.
4. If you commit a crime, you will be sent to prison.
5. Both the students were absent from the seminar, so their instructor was at a loss what to do.

**Chapter 6　冠詞(3)**
Ⅰ.
1. the
2. the, the
3. ×
4. the
5. ×

Ⅱ.
1. I met him by chance at the British Museum.
2. Last Sunday, we went to the school to play baseball.
3. We hired the boat by the hour.
4. She lives near Lake Biwa.
5. We sat in the shade of a beach umbrella.

Ⅲ.
1. The cherry-trees in Ueno Park are full in bloom, so why don't we go to see them at once?
2. Pencils are sold by the doze.
3. World War Ⅱ sustained heavy casualties.
4. The young are apt to misunderstand what the old say.
5. I would like to reserve a room at the Imperial Hotel.

Ⅳ.
1. He tried to climb Mt. Fuji, though he was lame in the left leg.
2. Walk along Oxford Street for a few minutes, and you will find the library in the right side.
3. We had been driving for three hours, when we saw a house in the distance.

4. He went to hospital the other day and had a doctor treat him for his fracture.
5. It goes without saying that the Japanese are a peace-loving people.

## Chapter 7　動詞(1)
I.
1. wore
2. tell
3. came
4. watching
5. rent

II.
1. If I find your watch, I will send it to you by post.
2. He once climbed the mountain some five years ago.
3. He got married to a French woman three years ago.
4. A man from China entered the room with a white coat on.
5. I began to feel like throwing up because of seasickness.

III.
1. I take this medicine every other day.
2. When he comes back from his European trip, I'll be at the airport to meet him.
3. The fine motion of the player wearing a blue shirt caught my eye.
4. Recently I have become so forgetful that I have to make a note of everything.
5. She plans to marry an American after she graduates from the university.

IV.
1. Please tell me your telephone number. I'll call you back.
2. Can you lend me ten thousand yen until payday?
3. We attended the meeting and demanded for a pay raise next year.
4. I used to get up early and take an hour's walk before breakfast.
5. Though I can't play baseball very well, I'm very fond of it. I make it a rule to enjoy it for some three hours on Sunday if it is not raining.

## Chapter 8　動詞(2)
I.
1. permit
2. have gone
3. remembered
4. chosen
5. opened

練習問題の解答　97

II.
1. He resembles his father, doesn't he?
2. I went to Tokyo last week.
3. I looked up his phone number in a telephone book.
4. He had his right leg injured in the traffic accident.
5. Our team beat the other team in the baseball game.

III.
1. He had his left leg wounded in the Civil War.
2. He is a great guy to be with, so I forgive him for telling a lie.
3. When and where is the next conference to be held?
4. I suddenly remembered that I had to look through a document to submit to the meeting.
5. The twins resemble each other so closely that we cannot tell one from the other.

IV.
1. He was selected for the prize from among hundreds of applicants.
2. When I arrived at the station, I noticed that my purse was missing.
3. He skipped his English class four times, so he couldn't get the credit of English.
4. When I got to the station, I found that the last train had already gone (left).
5. I have heard nothing from him for a long time. I wonder what has become of him.

## Chapter 9　形容詞
I.
1. You should gain as much knowledge as possible.
2. The number of the people here is much smaller than we expected.
3. She has fewer books than I have.
4. There was an enormous traffic jam in the downtown.
5. The car I bought yesterday is very expensive.

II.
1. hundred
2. a little
3. interesting
4. late
5. such

III.
1. The train left three minutes early.
2. I was thirty minutes late to the meeting because I missed the train by seconds.

3. He was really delighted to hear the good news.
4. "That bag must have been very expensive." "It wasn't. In fact, I bought it at a sale."
5. We didn't have much time then, so we went to the station by taxi.

Ⅳ.
1. I'm afraid that there is little time for argument.
2. This year there were few sunny days in June.
3. The foreigner spoke so fast that few of us could understand him.
4. Walk along that narrow street, and you will get to the station.
5. They were excited about traveling abroad for the first time.

**Chapter 10　副詞**
Ⅰ.
1. My father is much taller than I am.
2. If he doesn't go skating, I will not go, either.
3. He is much the best student in this class.
4. He has just done his homework.
5. My father usually takes a walk before breakfast.

Ⅱ.
1. enough
2. yet
3. heavily
4. hard
5. precisely

Ⅲ.
1. He was bold enough to speak ill of her in her presence.
2. He was too much excited to sleep that night.
3. I'm very tired of his long talk.
4. He could have easily been killed.
5. She is evidently the right person in the right place.

Ⅳ.
1. Frankly I don't think you need worry about that.
2. If you do not go, I shall not, either.
3. My hometown was so changed that I could hardly recognize it.
4. I have not even once caught cold for the past twenty years.
5. He despises the man simply because he is poorly dressed.

## Chapter 11　前置詞

Ⅰ.
1. during
2. to (with)
3. in
4. with
5. at

Ⅱ.
1. He called on the teacher during the summer vacation.
2. The second term begins in September.
3. The woman danced to the playing of the band till late at night.
4. The sun went down, but it remained light for about half an hour.
5. The train for Tokyo will start from this track in ten minutes.

Ⅲ.
1. The building will be completed by the end of this month.
2. I made friends with Jones during my stay in New York.
3. Are you going to the island by ship or by plane?
4. The train didn't come on time.
5. He died at his house on the morning of October 5, 1990.

Ⅳ.
1. My house is within a short walk from the station.
2. According to the report, twenty people were seriously injured in the traffic accident.
3. He suddenly came out from behind the wall.
4. I have been absent from school because of a cold for five days.
5. Would you come here again on Sunday afternoon at about three o'clock?

## Chapter 12　関係代名詞

Ⅰ.
1. His father has three sons, of whom he is the youngest.
2. I cannot remember the place where I left my coat.
3. I have done what you told me to do.
4. My father slipped on the ice, which we all laughed at.
5. The boy asked the reason why the teacher arrived late.

Ⅱ.
1. who
2. what

3. what
4. which
5. as
6. how
7. when
8. that
9. which
10. as

Ⅲ.
1. He is the only person in the world that can help me.
2. It was such a picture as he had never seen.
3. He does soon what he thinks is right.
4. He thought I was a doctor, which surprised me.
5. My hometown is almost the same as it was some ten years ago when I lived there.

Ⅳ.
1. I will come some other time when you are less busy.
2. There is hardly a rule but has an exception.
3. He was diligent, which his brother never was.
4. The way he spoke to us was suspicious.
5. I know nothing about the war beyond what I have read in the newspapers.

## Chapter 13　準動詞
Ⅰ.
1. reading
2. going
3. having
4. marrying
5. crawling
6. buried
7. Judging
8. written
9. trying
10. skating

Ⅱ.
1. I remember seeing the watch, but I have no idea where to look for it.
2. We are all looking forward to hearing the news of his marriage.
3. He promised to try hard, but he failed.

4. Badly injured in the leg, he could not walk any more.
5. The boy raising his left hand is our child.

Ⅲ.
1. He remembered to submit the document to the committee, but there were a few flaws in it.
2. I repented too late of having been idle when I was young.
3. Their conversation being in German, we could not understand what they were talking about.
4. The weather being fine, I kept the door open.
5. As I forgot to post this letter, my wife scolded me.

Ⅳ.
1. If you drive your car, you must carry your driving license with you.
2. Generally speaking, phonology is a fundamental field in linguistics.
3. On arriving at the door, he opened it soundlessly.
4. Don't speak with your mouth full.
5. He watched her dancing, never taking his eyes from her for a single moment.

## Chapter 14　比較

Ⅰ.
1. happiest
2. prettier
3. less
4. most difficult
5. longer, warmer

Ⅱ.
1. Baseball is preferable to football in our school.
2. He is three years senior to me.
3. He is worse off than he was five years ago.
4. The salesman is more wise than kind.
5. This picture is the better of the two he has painted.

Ⅲ.
1. This river is about half as broad as that river.
2. Though he is ten years junior to me, he knows well how to get along in life.
3. He is superior to me in academic achievement, but is inferior to me in experience.
4. You are as much to blame as he is.
5. He submitted a better paper than I expected.

Ⅳ.
1. He is better off than he used to be a few years ago.
2. When you are as old as I am, you will come to realize that it is necessary to see a lot of life.
3. I'm as grateful to him as to her.
4. Which of the two books is more useful in writing a paper?
5. This is the most impressive sight I have ever seen.

## Chapter 15　その他注意すべき構文
Ⅰ.
1. work
2. did I
3. dead
4. open
5. occur

Ⅱ.
1. I wonder when the letter will reach me.
2. You didn't attend the meeting and neither did I.
3. My brother and I would often go fishing.
4. She is proud of her long soft golden hair.
5. He had nothing particular to do yesterday.

Ⅲ.
1. Some rare pictures sell at a very high price.
2. The tiger which ran away from the zoo yesterday was caught alive.
3. Yesterday's cold weather turned the leaves red.
4. Never does he eat between meals.
5. He said that he had a lot of computer, but that he was not a computer nerd.

Ⅳ.
1. He took the intelligent old English artist for a clergyman.
2. I wonder what has become of the school where we studied in our childhood.
3. He and I are friends from college, but anyone who knows him will tell me he is a hard man to please.
4. It will rain tomorrow, for that mountain is covered by the cloud.
5. Is there anything interesting in today's paper?

練習問題の解答 103

語彙
1．日用品に関する語彙
1．②  2．⑨  3．⑧  4．④  5．③  6．⑩  7．⑥  8．①  9．⑦  10．⑤

2．文房具に関する語彙
1．⑨  2．⑩  3．⑧  4．②  5．③  6．④  7．⑦  8．⑤  9．①  10．⑥

3．食品に関する語彙
1．③  2．⑦  3．④  4．⑧  5．⑤  6．⑨  7．①  8．②  9．⑥  10．⑩

4．鉄道に関する語彙
1．④  2．⑤  3．⑩  4．②  5．⑦  6．⑧  7．①  8．⑥  9．③  10．⑨

5．犯罪に関する語彙(1)
1．⑤  2．⑩  3．④  4．⑥  5．③  6．①  7．⑨  8．⑦  9．⑧  10．②

6．犯罪に関する語彙(2)
1．②  2．⑥  3．⑨  4．③  5．④  6．⑩  7．①  8．⑤  9．⑦  10．⑧

7．犯罪に関する語彙(3)
1．②  2．⑤  3．④  4．⑦  5．⑧  6．③  7．①  8．⑩  9．⑨  10．⑥

8．科学技術に関する語彙
1．⑨  2．③  3．①  4．④  5．⑧  6．⑩  7．②  8．⑥  9．⑦  10．⑤

9．化学に関する語彙(1)
1．⑧  2．⑥  3．⑦  4．①  5．⑤  6．⑩  7．④  8．②  9．⑨  10．③

10．化学に関する語彙(2)
1．⑤  2．⑧  3．⑨  4．②  5．④  6．③  7．⑩  8．①  9．⑥  10．⑦

11．電話に関する語彙
1．③  2．⑧  3．⑨  4．⑤  5．①  6．⑩  7．②  8．⑥  9．⑦  10．④

12．気候に関する語彙(1)
1．⑨  2．⑤  3．⑧  4．③  5．②  6．⑦  7．④  8．⑩  9．①  10．⑥

13．気候に関する語彙(2)
1．⑦  2．⑨  3．⑥  4．⑧  5．②  6．③  7．⑤  8．⑩  9．①  10．④

14. 気候に関する語彙(3)
1. ⑥  2. ⑦  3. ⑤  4. ③  5. ④  6. ②  7. ①  8. ⑨  9. ⑩  10. ⑧

15. 郵便に関する語彙(1)
1. ⑩  2. ⑥  3. ⑧  4. ①  5. ②  6. ③  7. ⑦  8. ⑤  9. ⑨  10. ④

16. 郵便に関する語彙(2)
1. ⑨  2. ⑥  3. ④  4. ②  5. ⑤  6. ③  7. ⑧  8. ①  9. ⑩  10. ⑦

17. 郵便に関する語彙(3)
1. ⑧  2. ⑥  3. ⑤  4. ⑨  5. ②  6. ③  7. ①  8. ⑩  9. ⑦  10. ④

18. 学校に関する語彙(1)
1. ⑦  2. ⑥  3. ⑨  4. ⑩  5. ②  6. ④  7. ⑧  8. ⑤  9. ③  10. ①

19. 学校に関する語彙(2)
1. ⑩  2. ⑤  3. ②  4. ⑦  5. ⑧  6. ①  7. ⑥  8. ⑨  9. ④  10. ③

20. 学校に関する語彙(3)
1. ⑨  2. ⑧  3. ⑩  4. ③  5. ④  6. ⑦  7. ⑥  8. ⑤  9. ①  10. ②

21. 学問に関する語彙(1)
1. ⑨  2. ③  3. ⑦  4. ⑤  5. ⑧  6. ①  7. ⑩  8. ④  9. ⑥  10. ②

22. 学問に関する語彙(2)
1. ②  2. ⑥  3. ③  4. ⑧  5. ④  6. ⑨  7. ⑩  8. ⑤  9. ①  10. ⑦

23. 病名に関する語彙(1)
1. ⑥  2. ⑦  3. ⑧  4. ④  5. ⑩  6. ⑤  7. ②  8. ③  9. ①  10. ⑨

24. 病名に関する語彙(2)
1. ⑩  2. ①  3. ⑨  4. ⑥  5. ⑦  6. ②  7. ④  8. ⑤  9. ⑧  10. ③

25. 病名に関する語彙(3)
1. ⑨  2. ①  3. ⑦  4. ⑥  5. ⑧  6. ③  7. ⑩  8. ④  9. ②  10. ⑤

26. 医者に関する語彙
1. ②  2. ⑧  3. ⑩  4. ③  5. ①  6. ⑨  7. ⑥  8. ⑦  9. ⑤  10. ④

## 練習問題の解答

**27. 人体に関する語彙**
1. ②  2. ⑧  3. ⑨  4. ⑩  5. ⑦  6. ⑥  7. ④  8. ⑤  9. ①  10. ③

**28. 職業に関する語彙(1)**
1. ⑧  2. ⑨  3. ⑩  4. ⑥  5. ⑦  6. ④  7. ⑤  8. ②  9. ①  10. ③

**29. 職業に関する語彙(2)**
1. ⑨  2. ⑩  3. ④  4. ⑦  5. ①  6. ⑤  7. ③  8. ⑥  9. ⑧  10. ②

**30. 海外旅行に関する語彙(1)**
1. ⑥  2. ⑩  3. ⑨  4. ⑤  5. ⑦  6. ①  7. ②  8. ③  9. ④  10. ⑧

**31. 海外旅行に関する語彙(2)**
1. ②  2. ⑧  3. ⑨  4. ⑥  5. ⑦  6. ④  7. ⑩  8. ⑤  9. ①  10. ③

**32. 政治に関する語彙(1)**
1. ⑤  2. ⑩  3. ②  4. ⑨  5. ⑥  6. ④  7. ①  8. ③  9. ⑧  10. ⑦

**33. 政治に関する語彙(2)**
1. ⑤  2. ①  3. ⑨  4. ⑧  5. ⑥  6. ②  7. ④  8. ⑩  9. ⑦  10. ③

**34. 政治に関する語彙(3)**
1. ②  2. ④  3. ③  4. ⑤  5. ⑥  6. ①  7. ⑨  8. ⑩  9. ⑧  10. ⑦

**35. 政治に関する語彙(4)**
1. ⑦  2. ⑩  3. ⑧  4. ⑨  5. ③  6. ①  7. ④  8. ⑥  9. ②  10. ⑤

**36. 経済に関する語彙(1)**
1. ⑥  2. ④  3. ⑧  4. ⑩  5. ⑨  6. ⑦  7. ①  8. ②  9. ⑤  10. ③

**37. 経済に関する語彙(2)**
1. ③  2. ⑧  3. ①  4. ②  5. ⑥  6. ⑩  7. ④  8. ⑦  9. ⑤  10. ⑨

**38. 経済に関する語彙(3)**
1. ⑥  2. ⑤  3. ⑧  4. ⑩  5. ②  6. ③  7. ⑦  8. ⑨  9. ①  10. ④

**39. 宗教に関する語彙(1)**
1. ②  2. ⑨  3. ⑩  4. ⑦  5. ⑥  6. ⑧  7. ③  8. ①  9. ⑤  10. ④

40. 宗教に関する語彙(2)
1. ⑤  2. ⑨  3. ③  4. ④  5. ⑧  6. ⑦  7. ⑩  8. ⑥  9. ①  10. ②

41. ビジネスに関する語彙(1)
1. ⑦  2. ⑨  3. ⑥  4. ⑩  5. ⑤  6. ①  7. ②  8. ④  9. ⑧  10. ③

42. ビジネスに関する語彙(2)
1. ⑧  2. ⑨  3. ③  4. ④  5. ⑤  6. ⑩  7. ①  8. ⑦  9. ②  10. ⑥

43. ビジネスに関する語彙(3)
1. ④  2. ⑧  3. ①  4. ⑤  5. ⑥  6. ⑨  7. ⑩  8. ③  9. ⑦  10. ②

44. 図形に関する語彙(1)
1. ④  2. ③  3. ⑩  4. ①  5. ⑤  6. ⑦  7. ②  8. ⑥  9. ⑨  10. ⑧

45. 図形に関する語彙(2)
1. ③  2. ⑥  3. ⑦  4. ②  5. ④  6. ⑨  7. ⑧  8. ①  9. ⑤  10. ⑩

46. 数学に関する語彙(1)
1. ③  2. ⑥  3. ⑦  4. ①  5. ⑧  6. ⑩  7. ②  8. ⑤  9. ④  10. ⑨

47. 数学に関する語彙(2)
1. ⑧  2. ⑨  3. ①  4. ⑩  5. ⑤  6. ②  7. ④  8. ⑦  9. ⑥  10. ③

48. 数学に関する語彙(3)
1. ③  2. ②  3. ⑤  4. ①  5. ⑦  6. ④  7. ⑩  8. ⑧  9. ⑨  10. ⑥

49. 数学に関する語彙(4)
1. ⑥  2. ③  3. ⑤  4. ②  5. ⑩  6. ⑨  7. ①  8. ④  9. ⑧  10. ⑦

50. グラフに関する語彙
1. ③  2. ⑥  3. ⑨  4. ②  5. ④  6. ⑦  7. ⑤  8. ①  9. ⑩  10. ⑧

**著者略歴**

宗 正 佳 啓（むねまさ・よしひろ）

1963年山口県生まれ。2000年に九州大学大学院文学研究科より文学博士号を取得し，現在，福岡工業大学社会環境学部准教授。主な著書に *English Linguistics* 15 ("A Note on Tense Islands" の項執筆，開拓社，1998)，『言語学からの眺望2003』（「標準英語の非顕在的wh素性照合」の項執筆，九州大学出版会，2003)，*An Optimality Theoretic Approach to the C-system and its Cross-linguistic Variation*（九州大学出版会，2003)，*English Linguistics* 23 ("Notes on Covert *Wh*-agreement" の項執筆，開拓社，2006)，などがある。他論文多数。

---

英文法のポイント

2008年5月10日 初版発行
2011年4月1日 2刷発行

著　者　　宗　正　佳　啓
発行者　　五十川　直　行
発行所　　(財)九州大学出版会
　　　〒812-0053 福岡市東区箱崎7-1-146
　　　　　　　　九州大学構内
　　　　電話　092-641-0515(直通)
　　　　振替　01710-6-3677
　　　　　　　印刷・製本　大同印刷㈱

ⓒ 2008 Printed in Japan　　ISBN978-4-87378-968-2